I DON'T KNOW SH*T ABOUT HORSES

I DON'T KNOW SH*T ABOUT HORSES

BUT I SURE KNOW HOW TO SHOVEL IT

CANDY COVERDALE RODEWALD

Copyright © 2025
Candy Coverdale Rodewald

Performance Publishing
McKinney, TX

All Worldwide Rights Reserved.

All rights reserved. No part of this publication may be reproduced, stored in a retrieval system or transmitted, in any form or by any means, electronic, mechanical, recorded, photocopied, or otherwise, without the prior written permission of the copyright owner, except by a reviewer who may quote brief passages in a review.

I have explained the tricks in this book to help readers better understand how they are performed. Please do not attempt these on your own without the guidance of a professional trick rider and a properly trained trick riding horse. Some skills can be introduced using a fiberglass or metal horse. However, all tricks performed on a horse are extremely dangerous, and even experienced trick riders can sustain serious injuries or be fatally harmed.

ISBN: 978-1-961781-69-6 (paperback)

CONTENTS

Acknowledgment ix
Introduction..xi

Chapter 1 – 1947-1955..1
    Where It All Began..1
    An Animal-loving Asthmatic 3

Chapter 2 – Arizona: mid-1950s – 1967 7
    Horse-Crazy Sisters 8
    Termite 10
    My Introduction to Rodeos and Trick Riding...............11

Chapter 3 – Trick Rider 15
    Trick Roping 22
    J.W. Stoker 22
    An Early Life Lesson: Don't Give Unsolicited Advice 24

Chapter 4 – Special Horses, Dogs, and People....................27
    Hobo: 1964 - Going Home from Salinas, CA 28
    Playboy the Palomino..30
    Chipper..37
    Taco & The Clowns 41

Chapter 5 – Independent Cowgirl (with a little help).................45
    Fort Smith, Arkansas to Kansas City, Missouri -
        Tornado 1966 45

  January 1967 - Denver Stock Show 47
  1966-67 - A Story About Lawrence Tenny Stevens
   (1896-1972) 52

Chapter 6 – The Love of My Life - Roy Rodewald 57

Chapter 7 – Livingston, Montana 1968 67

Chapter 8 – The Cow Palace 1968 73

Chapter 9 – 1969 - 1973 81
  MEXICO, HERE WE COME! Spring 1972 82

Chapter 10 – Winding Down Our Rodeo Careers 93
  Change Your Plan 103

Chapter 11 – A Tribute to My Special Friend, Connie Griffith ...107
  Connie Griffith Story #1: Over the Mountain 109
  Connie Griffith Story #2: Road Block 112

Chapter 12 – Bad News Bob, the Redneck Schnauzer—
 Also known as Biblical Bob 117

Chapter 13 – 2013—Something I Did That Was Bad 127

Chapter 14 – Pony Cart Wreck #1—January 2013 133

Chapter 15 – Reinventing Myself 139
  December 2019—Waco the Miniature Horse (from
   Waco's perspective) 141

Chapter 16 – On the Road Again With Eleven Angels 145
 Oh No! Pony Cart Wreck #2 156

Chapter 17 – The Basics of Riding as Related to My Faith 159

Chapter 18 – Conclusion 163
 Putting My Insights into the Basics 163

A Simplified History of Trick Riding..165
Scoring Sheet 169
Rodeo Performers I Performed With 177
Life Story Time Line 181

ACKNOWLEDGMENT

I praise the Lord for my life and the wonderful family with whom I have been blessed.

I dedicate this book to the love of my life, my husband Roy, who kept my life exciting throughout our marriage. He went to be with the Lord in 2001.

I want to express my gratitude to the many people who contributed to my book and my life.

Thanks to Tad Griffith for helping me with the special stories about his mom, Connie.

Thanks to my sister, Anita Paulson, and my niece, Laura Lyons, for helping me correct various mistakes in my writing.

I am also grateful to everyone included in these stories, whose life lessons made my own life richer and more interesting.

I appreciate the assistance of my publisher, Michelle Prince of Performance Publishing, for guiding me through the publishing and editing process.

Lastly, I thank my granddaughter, Sierra, for her work on my old photos to make them acceptable to the publisher.

INTRODUCTION

My life was shaped by horses. Good ones, great ones, bad ones… and the ones I should have done better by. Each one taught me life lessons, moved my life in new directions, took me places, and led me to people who would shape who I am.

After working with horses for over sixty years as a professional trick rider, barrel racer, competing in horse shows, hunter-jumper, and dressage, studying natural horsemanship, and heeling cattle with my husband, Roy, I have learned it never hurts to review what I used to know and have forgotten. It now physically hurts or is even impossible to do what I used to do, and I no longer ride. However, even after a lifetime, there is still more to learn. Just like life.

I have a quote from Roy Rodgers hanging in my garage that reads, *"When you are young and you get bucked off, you may break something, but when you are my age, you splatter."* I try to help others by sharing what knowledge I have. I believe we are blessed to be a blessing. The stories in this book are true. I hope you enjoy them and learn from my many mistakes.

What I've come to know, as I near the end of my life, is that I don't know shit about horses, but I sure know how to shovel it.

-Candy Rodewald
Author

CHAPTER 1
1947-1955

Where It All Began

Of all the children in my family, I was the least likely to have a career with animals. I was born on June 20, 1947, in Chicago, Illinois, the last of four children of Leora Lettie Alaxson-Coverdale and William Albert Coverdale. My parents were weary and lacking imagination by the time I arrived, so Nancy, my oldest sibling by twenty years, chose my name. She called me Candace, with the 'ace' ending like the Candace in the Bible. My family nicknamed me Candy. Nancy got married when I was almost three years old.

Candy's sister, Nancy, kissing her on her wedding day

No one could think of a middle name for the new baby. That was left for me to choose at the time of my baptism in the Methodist church. I chose Dale after my then idol Dale Evans. So, I was Candace Dale Coverdale.

My brother, Bill, fifteen years my senior, once confided in me, "You should have seen the look on Mom's face when she found out she was going to have you." He did not indicate it was a face filled with joy. My youngest sister, Anita, often filled the role of my mother, as she was ten years older than me.

In 1947, the year I was born, President Harry Truman forecasted a budget surplus, Stanford University isolated the polio virus, the cost of a new house averaged $6,650.00, and a car $1,290.00. A gallon of gas was fifteen cents, and the average income was $2,854.00.

My memories of Chicago are few as I was about three years old when we moved to Waterford, Wisconsin, and then to Racine, WI. Even at that age, I had a love for animals and a dislike for dolls, much to my mother's dismay. She was a housewife and had devoted her life to staying home and raising us kids, and this was beyond her grasp of reality. She would dutifully buy me a doll at Christmas time, and I would always reject it and gravitate toward anything that had to do with animals. She finally got the message after I threw one of my dolls against the wall, shattering it to pieces.

In Racine, I had a very nice baby stroller where I kept a small beanbag named Freddy the Frog. Freddy was a gift from my mother's friend, Dorothy, who must have sensed that a frog would be more appreciated by me than a doll. Freddy was always a surprise to those who were anxious to see my beautiful doll in the fancy stroller, peeking in only to see a small bean bag frog.

An Animal-loving Asthmatic

Unfortunately, I was severely allergic to any animal that had hair on it. After having to give up a kitten shortly after acquiring it, my pets became those without hair—turtles and goldfish. When they would die. I would cry for days and bury them underneath the porch of our apartment building in Racine. I was six-or seven years old years old the summer I had to bury my precious turtle. The kids in the neighborhood made fun of me. I believe they thought I was overreacting to the death of my small turtle, and when they dug him up and hid him from me, I was heartbroken.

One time, after much begging, my dad took me fishing across the street in Racine, off the pier in Lake Michigan. I caught a small fish and placed him in a bucket of water, where I found him dead the following morning. I cried my eyes out over that fish and swore I would never go fishing again. My kind father comforted me and supported me in my decision. I admit to being a hypocrite as I can eat fish and other animals, but I can't kill them.

I was very shy as a child. I remember when my cousins from Wisconsin came to visit us, I would hide behind the couch until I was coaxed out to play with them. I have worked hard through the years to overcome that shyness. I have learned that if I look at a person with love and focus on them instead of my fears and problems, I can forget about being shy.

It was common for people to smoke in those days, and the idea of how harmful the smoke could be was not yet common knowledge. Both of my parents smoked indoors. My mom didn't start smoking until she became pregnant with me. Her incentive was to keep her weight down. They didn't understand how much of a toll that habit would take on my health and their lives. I don't know at what age I became ill with asthma, but I did miss all of kindergarten and most of first grade because of it.

When I would have an asthma attack, I would start to panic as I would wheeze, cough, and could barely breathe. These attacks landed me in the hospital for a week or more at a time, especially during the winter months. The times I remember most were Thanksgiving and Christmas. It was lonely in the hospital. I remember getting shots of penicillin three times a day.

I also remember a very nice elderly lady who came to visit me occasionally and brought me a mini copy of the New Testament. I still have it.

I don't remember ever being in the hospital in the summer in Wisconsin. I was always outside in the summer, away from the cigarette smoke.

The Doctors did not predict a very good outcome for me in Wisconsin and encouraged my parents that I would do much better in Arizona.

CHAPTER 2
ARIZONA: MID-1950S — 1967

The summer before I began second grade, my parents decided to move to Arizona to help my health. A concerned boss offered Dad a job in Phoenix near Scottdale as a government inspector at Motorola Research, and I was registered to start school at La Loma Elementary in Scottsdale. My oldest siblings had already left home, so it was just Mom, Dad, Anita, and I, boarding the train for the three-day adventure to Scottsdale.

I was old enough to understand that it was a sacrifice for Mom and Dad to leave the Midwest, which had been their home since birth, but young enough for a long train ride to be exciting. We had a room on the train to sleep in. Having been nowhere, but with a healthy imagination, I envisioned the train being attacked by outlaws like in Western movies. Fortunately, all went well on our journey.

Severe bronchitis and asthma continued to plague me for the first couple of years in Arizona. I frequented Good Samaritan Hospital in Phoenix on most holidays. I tested positive for dust and animal hair, and the indoor smoking aggravated my lungs even more. But, by fourth grade, I was finally starting to see the beginning of a healthier existence, aided, I believe, by the fact that I could spend most of my time year-round outside, away from cigarette smoke. After two years, even the Arizona dust and animal hair bothered me less. Finally, I could be around animals without suffering so severely, and my greatest passion became horses.

Horse-Crazy Sisters

We lived within walking distance from Casa Blanca Stables, where I would hang out and work—cleaning stalls, grooming horses, and doing any other jobs that would earn me a ride on a horse. One time, before a parade in Scottsdale, Mom was surprised to find the stagecoach harness from the stables in our bathtub, waiting to be polished. It was a big deal for me then to be able to ride in the Scottsdale parade. It lost its luster in later years when, as a professional trick rider, it became a requirement in all the rodeos I worked at.

On Donkey with future hopes

I eventually worked my way up to being a guide for the trail rides. Casa Blanca and my house were both East of Camelback Mountain. I enjoyed the breathtaking view of Camelback Mountain, riding the many desert trails. Not a bad job for a high school kid. If I worked all day, I would get paid with lunch at Casa Blanca and, of course, the chance to ride horses all day.

Termite

My dad's friend had two horses. When Sam heard that Dad's daughters were horse crazy, he was kind enough to allow us to ride them. I was ecstatic. This was before Anita was a Rodeo Queen's attendant, so I was probably in third grade. A beautiful, spirited white horse was assigned to Anita. I got to ride sixteen-hand-high Termite, who was gentler. We enjoyed several successful rides. I rode with a Mexican saddle, which had a characteristic very wide horn that I could not get my hand around.

One beautiful evening, we saddled up for a ride in the gorgeous desert. At one point on our ride, I remember a black cat running in front of us. It made the horses a little nervous, but they didn't panic. I didn't think much of it then, but after the next events of the evening, I became superstitious about black cats for many years.

It was twilight as we headed back to the barn, and the wind was picking up and blowing branches off the trees. We were riding past Judson school, a private school with a polo field, when Termite suddenly panicked and bolted. We never knew the cause of his spook. It was summer, so the school was closed and deserted. Perhaps he was hit by a branch blowing in the wind.

Whatever the cause, he started running towards his barn. I was petrified and clung to that saddle as best as I could, although I couldn't get a good grip on that big horn. Anita knew not to run after Termite as he would think he was in a horse race and ran faster. She watched him duck around the corner of a barn that had a heavy growth of trees around it with me on him and come out the other side without me on him. Anita hurried to see what happened to me. She found me on the polo field, disoriented, but not knocked out.

She instructed me to stay there and remounted her horse to go as fast as she could to get Dad. They soon returned with the car to rush me to Good Samaritan Hospital in Phoenix.

I was diagnosed with a severe concussion and a broken ear drum and instructed to not ride a horse for at least a year. It was questionable, but I made it through the night.

When I awoke the next morning, Mom was by my side. The first thing I asked her was, "Mom, will you let me ride Termite again?"

She shook her finger in my face and said, "You will never ride a horse again."

I was crushed, but true to the doctor's orders, she did not let me ride again for a full year.

My Introduction to Rodeos and Trick Riding

Anita became a Rodeo Queen's Attendant at the Phoenix Rodeo when I was in fourth grade. It was a blessing as she included me in most of the activities, which included dressing in the part of a stylish cowgirl and attending every rodeo event that year. Watching my sister ride with the Rodeo Royalty, handing out awards to the rugged cowboys and cowgirls, and fulfilling her duties of connecting fans with the rodeo world was exciting. The experience enlarged my dream of one day being a trick rider.

I started saving every cent I could for a Dick Griffith Trick Riding Saddle. Porters Saddle Shop sold the saddle. The price was $375.00. After several years, I had only managed to save $150.00.

I was a Sophomore at Scottsdale High School when I learned that Fern Seminoff was teaching trick riding at Seminoff Stable, a well-run local boarding and training stable. She charged $10.00 per lesson, so I decided to use my hard-earned $150.00 on fifteen lessons. It proved to be a worthwhile investment as it launched my trick riding career. I was able to walk to the stables from school, and my dad would pick me up on his way home from work. When I ran out of money, I cleaned her house and trained the horses that were eventually sold to her students. She would sell the horse to a student, then I would have to train a new one for my next rodeo.

Fern excelled at teaching showmanship, which fit me to a T. For the first time, I found something I excelled at, and under Fern's guidance, confidence replaced my old shyness. She taught me to have the fluidity and grace of a dancer, the polish and grooming of a performer, and added colorful costumes, speed, and excitement to round it out. Learning showmanship brought out my personality, and when I was on a horse, it was easy to smile and show off a bit, to have fun, and to revel in the attention I received rather than hide in the shadows of shyness.

Trick roping by Rondo – first horse

Fern also helped me overcome my fear of running horses, a remnant of my accident with Termite, years earlier. Trick riders perform with their horses in a dead run, which is appealing to the audience. If I wanted to be a trick rider, it was a fear I had to get over, and I did.

CHAPTER 3
TRICK RIDER

I was fifteen years old when I performed at my first rodeo in Scottsdale, in February 1963. I would be riding with some of the trick riding greats, such as Edith Happy, May Boss, and Mary Stetler. These ladies were not only trick riders but also worked as stunt riders in movies. It was such a privilege to ride with them on my first professional rodeo, February of my sophomore year in high school.

CANDY COVERDALE RODEWALD

Roping on Rondo, 1963

I was ecstatic, but so nervous. I ate very little the day before, or the day of the rodeo. I had been practicing my trick riding every day, and I knew the tricks well. Still, I was nervous about putting on performances, and I struggled with that old shy side. But the minute

I turned my horse around for the first run, the nervousness transformed into effort, and my desire to make the audience happy and give them the thrill they had come for took over.

The main tricks I used were The Hippodrome Stand, Cossack Drag, Stroud Lay Out, Tail Drag, Half-Shoulder Stand, Full Fender, and Backbend. (See index for full description of these tricks)

Liberty Stand with ropes, Ft. Smith AR 1965

I DON'T KNOW SH*T ABOUT HORSES

Full Fender on Chipper, Imperial CA

Candy stands twirling ropes, Salinas

Back bend on Hobo

Behind the scenes was my mom. She had never approved of my addiction to horses, especially after my wreck on Termite, even though she grew up on a farm and used to ride the plow horse so her dad would have someone to keep him company when he plowed the fields. But my riding did allow her to fulfill a dream of being a costume designer. My mother seldom watched me ride. She usually partially covered her eyes with her fingers to do so. She did a beautiful job designing and sewing my costumes and she enjoyed the praise she received for her talent.

I remember my mother washing clothes in our wringer washer in the utility room behind the carport. The clean clothes went through the wringer into the rinse sink, then through the wringer again to be hung out on our very fancy rotating square clothesline. In the Arizona heat, by the time the last piece of clothing was fastened to the line, the first piece was dry and ready to be taken down. It was much faster than today's modern dryers.

Edith Happy liked my riding and got me contracts to ride at all of Andy Jauregui's Rodeos in Arizona and California with them. Andy was a stock contractor, responsible for supplying the bucking horses, bulls, calves, and steers for the rodeo, and also the contract acts. These included the trick riders, horse and dog acts, the Rodeo Clowns, the announcer, and the rodeo secretary. He organized the grand entry and usually participated in the parade. He was the one who was hired to run the show, and to get a contract in his shows was a big deal.

One of the most special things about that time was the many famed trick riders I rode with. I trick rode with J.W. Stoker and Bill and JoAnn McEnany the summer I graduated from High School. Before I had my own vehicle, I would trick ride at several rodeos with one group, using their horses. When it was time to join another group, I'd pack up my saddle and take the bus to meet them, where I'd ride their horses for the next set of rodeos. I made enough money that summer to buy a new 1965 Chevy half-ton pick-up for $2,100.00. By then, I had graduated from High School. I was soon on the road in my own vehicle.

I was blessed to also ride with Vernon Nichols, Janette Plunkett, Karen Womack/Vold, Rex & Wanda Rossi, Connie & Tad Griffith and many more. It was an amazing time in my life.

Trick Roping

I had the ambition to be a trick rider starting about fourth grade. However, at that age, I lacked the resources to get a horse of my own, a trick riding saddle, or an instructor. But I could afford a trick rope, so I began to learn trick roping. It can be very frustrating without a teacher, but I did persevere and learned some tricks. They would come in handy in time, because once I proceeded into the world of trick riding, I used my trick roping skills to do publicity for the rodeos I trick rode at, usually at public events or for TV interviews.

Following my idol, Nancy Shepard, who retired before I became a trick rider, I often spun a rope in each hand like she did while I stood on the horse, as it made my stand more unique than others doing the same trick.

J.W. Stoker

I started trick riding with J.W. Stoker in 1965. When he called to ask me to trick ride with him, I didn't have a car, so I would take the bus to meet him at a rodeo, and I would travel with Karen Atterberry who also worked with him to the rodeos. I also worked with Bill and JoAnne McEnany and rode a paint horse of theirs. When I switched between the two groups, I would pack my saddle up and ride the bus to a new location.

He also did trick roping, and he helped me with my roping skills. I often helped him by holding his horse while he was performing, and occasionally I got to participate in it by trick roping. I started out by holding his horse for him when he completed his Texas Skip—twirling the rope sideways and jumping through it as he made it go from side to side.

Ride n Rock Ranch, Scottsdale AZ

He used a white horse called Prissy for his roping act. He allowed me to ride her for trick riding when I worked with him. She would get pretty excited when they began playing *Deep in The Heart of Texas* because she knew that J.W. would soon run toward her, grab the 6" trick riding horn, and she could take off running as he vaulted onto the saddle. I usually got dragged by Prissy a few feet before J.W. was able to catch up with her. Under his breath, he would warn me not to let go of her as he ran toward her.

I only really messed up on my duties once, and fortunately, it was at a practice session at the Denver Stock Show. They had the Contract

Acts Convention back in those days just before the rodeo in Denver. One evening after the convention, we headed over to the rodeo grounds so J.W. could practice his act with the music one time before the rodeo. I was still in my dress and high heels from the convention. It was cold, and Prissy had not worked for the four days we were at the convention, so she was feeling pretty fresh. She jumped into a run as her favorite song began to play, jerking me off my feet and dragging me a ways before I finally had to let go. I could hear J.W. exclaiming, "Don't let go of her!" as I was being dragged down the arena. Fortunately, it was just a practice, and no one was any worse for wear.

J.W. trained many trick riders and ropers during his career, and the 'King of the Cowboy Trick Ropers and Riders' was inducted into the National Cowboy Hall of Fame in 1999, the Texas Cowboy Hall of Fame in 2007, the Pro Rodeo Hall of Fame in 2011, and the Texas Rodeo Cowboy Hall of Fame in 2015. He passed away at the age of ninety-four in 2022, a rodeo legend.

An Early Life Lesson: Don't Give Unsolicited Advice

Gary Gist was handsome, talented, and well-off, and I had a date with him! We had gotten acquainted at the summer rodeos when I was seventeen. I was a trick rider, and he was a top team roper. He heeled with his dad, Byron, qualifying to compete in the National Finals Rodeo many times. They won it in 1964, roping together.

I was still attending Scottsdale High School in Arizona, and he was in town for the rodeo. I always looked forward to having some fun when dancing. I never drank alcohol, but I loved to dance, and Gary was a fantastic dancer.

He pulled up to my parents' house in his white Cadillac. When I entered the car, the white tuck-and-roll leather upholstery welcomed me. I settled into the comfortable front seat beside him. Then, I became aware of the rock and roll music playing on the radio. I thought to myself, this cowboy, being from California, doesn't know where the country music channels are here in Arizona.

"We have some great country stations here," I remarked. "Let me find one for you." I leaned toward the radio to assist in finding one for him.

He cleared his throat and sternly said, "It's a record player."

Record player

This was definitely a bad move on my part. I didn't even know such a thing existed for cars. I learned a lot from Gary Gist. Every time I put on one of my many barrel racing trophy buckles made by his family's company GIST Buckles, I think fondly of Gary.

CHAPTER 4
SPECIAL HORSES, DOGS, AND PEOPLE

Starflyers, 1964

CANDY COVERDALE RODEWALD

Hobo: 1964 - Going Home from Salinas, CA

Hobo was a beautiful black horse—one of the few I trusted enough to do a backbend on. I had trained him for trick riding, then purchased him.

My dad and I had spent a great weekend at the Salinas Rodeo, where I trick rode and everything had gone well. We were on our way home on a packed, two-lane highway late Sunday afternoon. I had my driver's permit (not my full license), and my dad was letting me drive his 1959 Ford Fairlane hardtop convertible with a heavy two-horse, straight-load trailer pulling behind.

Everything was going fine until a car driving from the opposite direction decided he could pass a line of cars. He was at high speed, coming head-on toward me. I slammed on the brakes and the trailer started swaying from right to left. We didn't have trailer brakes at that time, which didn't help the situation. Hobo was tied in with the halter rope and fell hard against the tailgate with his back end, breaking it open and falling out of the trailer and dragging his back legs on the pavement before I came to a full stop. The driver of the car veered past me, barely missed hitting me, and drove off the road on the right side of our car.

Several people stopped to help, and the highway patrol arrived shortly after. One witness said the man slid to a stop, got out, walked around his car to see if it was damaged, got back in, made a left turn back on the highway, and continued his journey.

I was in distress. Hobo's back legs were cut almost to the bone at the front of the bend in his lower leg. With help from the highway patrol, a veterinarian, and many others, we had the tailgate fixed, Hobo bandaged and loaded in the trailer, and we continued to our first night's stop, just south of Los Angelas, CA. The vet had given Hobo plenty of pain medication, so he traveled well.

My dad took over the driving from that point on. I was brokenhearted and shed many tears. We got home the next day and started the long rehab for Hobo. I would halter him every day and rode a borrowed horse for three months to lead him an hour a day to help his recovery. He seemed to heal well, and I eventually started riding him again. I used him in two more rodeos before he became permanently lame as a result of the accident, and the vet recommended we put him to sleep because he would always be in pain. Another broken heart for me.

Hobo, Salinas 1964

Back bend on Hobo, Salinas 1964

Playboy the Palomino

I was without a horse with some rodeos on the horizon.

Dick Dunnigan and James J. Dunnigan, were here from the East Coast to establish a new trotting track in Goodyear, near Phoenix. James had successfully founded harness racing tracks in New York and California, and he felt Arizona was ready to get in on the action.

Dick, who was in his late teens or early twenties, kept his horse, Playboy, at Seminoff's stable, where I trick rode. Playboy was a beautiful palomino Quarter horse, about fifteen-two hands high. He was a half-brother to Trigger, Roy Rodger's horse.

Candy on Playboy

He was already trained to do tricks of his own. He would rear on command and shake hands with you, but one trick he did caused a problem for me. He would lay down on command, and Playboy could lay down at speed when given the cue.

Candy Cossack Drag, Lawton OK 1965

I didn't see a lot of Dick around the stable, but when I did always supportive and helpful, and eventually, he offered chance to use Playboy for trick riding. Playboy was sweet a ant of me as I did my tricks on him, except for the tail drag seemed to enjoy his new job.

Playboy and Candy, 1965

Candy Coverdale, Stroud Layout Salinas 1966

One of my tricks, the Fender Drag, involved sliding down the side of the saddle and tucking my knee under the fender of the saddle, then leaning my weight back so that I was lying beside the left side of the horse's body. That action seemed to be close enough to his cue that he thought he should lay down and he would immediately stop and drop to the ground. This was very inconvenient considering, I was what he would lay down on. Fortunately, I was able to swing up from my hanging position and jump off of him before I got hurt. My first project was to un-train him from doing that. I would slip down his side and tap him with the whip so he continued running. He learned not to lie down at speed in a short time.

The person who had taught him all his fancy tricks had likely never used him at speed very much, and he didn't have a very good whoa at the end of my runs. Because of this, I sometimes needed to use the fence to stop him. Andy Jauregui gave me a spade bit, which is more severe and produced a more solid whoa at the end of my runs, saving Andy the need of fixing his fences every time I rode.

I used Playboy at several rodeos before I got another horse. He was a pleasure, and he taught me a lot.

I DON'T KNOW SH*T ABOUT HORSES

Republic Photo by Ed Ryan

UNCLE MILTIE'S IN TOWN—Candy Coverdale, 17, of Scottsdale was at the airport yesterday to give Milton Berle an assist with breakfast. Another Milton—Mayor Graham—was on hand to proclaim the entertainer an official Phoenix ambassador of goodwill. And police officer Richard Mullins was on hand to stick the Berle car with an overtime parking ticket. Uncle Miltie will star in the broadway hit, "Never Too Late," opening Feb. 9 at the Sombrero Playhouse.

Candy with Uncle Miltie

CANDY COVERDALE RODEWALD

Uncle Miltie, 1965

I DON'T KNOW SH*T ABOUT HORSES

Chipper

It was 1965, and I was seventeen years old. I had a show in two weeks at the Yuma Arizona Rodeo, and, of course, my horse, Hobo, came up lame. His old injuries from the trailer accident were catching up with him.

Candy with Cotton Rosser, Nephi UT

Vernon had booked a separate show with another girl, but she had backed out, so he asked me to take her place. It was an amazing opportunity to work with one of the best. Vernon had made an agreement with the rodeo that hired him that we would do one run without bridles. I needed a horse, and fast!

I had moved my horse to a new stable on the canal in Scottsdale, run by Joe Samsill, the brand inspector. A couple of guys that I didn't know had heard about my dilemma had a horse they thought might work for me and they brought him out for me to try.

Upside-down on Chipper, Imperial CA 1965

Chipper was a big bay gelding who had a lot of fear in him. He needed a tie down on or he would rear over backwards. I brought him to the arena and showed him the straightaway pattern a few times and decided to give him the real test. He liked to run, so that wasn't a problem. I turned him around and dropped into a tail drag, with my feet held into straps at the back of the saddle, my legs around his rump, and my fingertips dragging in the dirt behind him. Joe told me, later, that he almost fainted when I did that. Chipper didn't lose his mind or kick my head in, so he passed the test and became my new trick riding mount.

Candy on Chipper, Imperial CA 1965

Vernon and I performed at Yuma, AZ, and Imperial, CA without a bridle, two weeks later. I used Chipper for the rest of that year, and he became more confident with each show. He lost his fear, so he no longer ran in panic mode. He developed an interesting habit that made the audience gasp. When I was in a tail drag and would tighten my leg muscles to basically do a sit-up to get back in the saddle, he would buck and throw me back in the saddle.

It made a great finish.

Candy on Chipper, 1965

Candy Tail Drag on Chipper, Ft. Smith AR 1966

I DON'T KNOW SH*T ABOUT HORSES

Taco & The Clowns

I like my horses big and my dogs little. I always loved animals of all sizes, but small dogs are easier to travel with and make less of a mess. I love horses of all sizes. The horse I currently have is big at sixteen hands tall (a hand is a 4-inch measurement), but the smaller horses are becoming more appealing as I age.

It was 1966, and I was headed to trick ride the rodeo in Omaha, Nebraska. AKSARBEN was what they called —that's Nebraska spelled backwards. Traveling alone got pretty lonely, and when I saw a sign at a farm along the way that said Chihuahua Puppies for Sale, I immediately put on the brakes and pulled into the farmhouse to purchase one. I picked a brown and white spotted puppy, and I was on our way to the rodeo with my new little friend.

Candy and Taco

I had been told that in Mexico, they often used their dogs as food, and I figured she would provide enough meat for a few tacos, so I named her Taco.

The AKSARBEN rodeo had ten performances. One of the acts was known as the Beer Box Act.

One rodeo clown would have a box filled with beer bottles. Another clown would pretend to want a beer, so he would chase the first clown, grab the box, and trip, supposably breaking the bottles inside. Beer would start pouring out of the corner of the box. The clown who had stolen the box would lift the box and guzzle down the liquid streaming from the corner. They'd set the box down and a dog would jump out. For this rodeo, the clowns needed a dog for their act. The dog they used, of course, was my new puppy, Taco.

After that, if you approached Taco and your pants were baggie, she would growl at you. She hated clowns or anyone with loose pants at the bottom for the rest of her life.

CHAPTER 5
INDEPENDENT COWGIRL (WITH A LITTLE HELP)

Fort Smith, Arkansas to Kansas City, Missouri - Tornado 1966

I had just finished performing at the Fort Smith, AR Night Rodeo and needed to be in Kansas City in a couple of days, so I needed to get a good start. My days of hitchhiking with J.W. and other trick riders were over as I had now purchased my first truck and trailer, and I spent a lot of time on my own on the rodeo trail. My parents were concerned, but they supported me and didn't protest too much, as long as I called them frequently to let them know I was okay. We had no cell phones back then, so I had to call collect from a pay phone. I was young and naïve, and by the grace of God, I never had trouble with people who meant me harm. In fact, it was often the opposite, and most people I met were incredibly kind and helpful.

Postcard sent to home

Candy's postcard sent to home

On this occasion, I loaded Chipper into my one-horse trailer behind my new '65 Chevy half-ton pick-up with a topper on it and we headed north. It started to rain, and as I drove further north, the rain got more serious and lightning lit up the sky, making the drive more than a little frightening. I was always very tense when I was driving, careful to avoid accidents, but this time was far worse. In the flashes of light, I could see many tornadoes that were a part of this storm.

I was terrified and pulled into a farmhouse to ask if I could shelter my horse Chipper in their barn. I told them I would sleep in the camper topper, but they insisted I sleep in their house. I'll never forget their generosity or the relief I felt to get off the road that night.

I was blessed to receive help from so many people on my journeys as a teenager traveling alone

January 1967 - Denver Stock Show

I was excited and in a hurry to get to the Denver Stock show to trick ride with J.W. Stoker. I was going to use his beautiful white horse, Prissy, to trick ride on.

Candy on Prissy, Ft. Smith AR

I was between horses at that time, and there was a horse being brought there for me to consider as my next trick riding horse. I hooked up my empty one-horse trailer to start my journey north from Arizona so I could transport the new horse home should I choose to buy it. A huge snowstorm had passed through northern Arizona and New Mexico and had delayed my departure, so I was eager to get on the road. I had little experience with the after-effects of a snowstorm, having lived most of my life in warm Scottsdale. I started early in the morning with a goal to get to Gallup, NM, to spend the night.

The beautiful, sunny day started out well. Just south of Flagstaff, a scene I was not familiar with came into view—it was called snow-packed roads. I had never driven on such a thing and was extremely careful. I somehow made it through Flagstaff and was headed east toward Gallup when the snowpack dissipated. It was sunny again and there were clear roads for many miles.

Suddenly, things changed. Several miles west of a town called Sanders, AZ I encountered black ice (clear, solid, nearly invisible ice) for the first time in my life. The snow had melted the previous day and refroze the night before, turning the road into a skating rink, and by the time I arrived late that morning, it was beginning to melt again. It looked like a Zamboni had just finished polishing. I scrambled to remember what I had studied about driving on ice. *Don't step on the brakes. Turn in the direction of the skid.* That was working pretty well as I skidded off the right side of the road. Fortunately, it was open and flat.

That suddenly deteriorated when I saw a deep culvert directly ahead of me. I slammed on my brakes, spun in a circle, and my truck ended up lying on its right side. Poor little Taco, the Chihuahua, was terrified on the passenger side against the door. The horse trailer, fortunately with no horse in it, followed far enough behind that the hitch was broken but it was still upright.

The Highway Patrol soon showed up and helped Taco and me get out of the overturned truck. By then, vehicles were sliding off both sides of the highway. One vehicle had a carload of High School basketball players that went off the road into the culvert. One of them broke an arm, but it could have been so much worse. No one was killed.

My horse trailer was eventually hauled to Gallup to have the broken hitch rewelded. They set my truck upright and hauled it to the gas station in Sanders to get the oil changed. Another lesson learned! When you turn a vehicle over, you need to get the oil changed or the engine might seize. The snow was so deep where the truck landed that it didn't even break the mirror, and no harm was done.

One of the kind officers took me to the gas station where my truck was being towed for the oil change. He then took me to a nearby restaurant for an early dinner. By the time my truck was ready, and I returned to the gas station, it was late. I asked the gas station owner if he would mind if I parked there and slept in my camper topper overnight. He said it would be better for me to sleep in the room attached to the back of the gas station. The owner was a Mormon missionary living in a house nearby with his large family. He was planning on building a church there on the Indian reservation.

I have driven by Sanders since then. The gas station, although still there, is closed, but there is a large, newer Mormon church nearby. I frequently think of the kindness of that family in Sanders. In all reality, they probably saved my life as it was twenty below zero that night. I would have either frozen to death or killed myself using the portable propane heater in my camper.

The next morning, I chained up my truck and headed to Gallup to pick up my trailer to continue my journey. I kept those chains on all the way to Denver, even for the many miles I did not need them. I was thankful to not be hauling a horse.

Candy on Budweiser horse, Denver 1966

1966-67 - A Story About Lawrence Tenny Stevens (1896-1972)

Lawrence Tenny Stevens was a great sculptor. We called him Steve. He was in the process of doing a rodeo series that Valley National Bank in Arizona had commissioned him to do. I was young and enjoyed some recognition in the field of trick riding when Steve got in contact with me. He told me he was doing a series on Rodeo and was planning to do a Trick Rider and asked if I would help. I was, of course, very flattered and couldn't be more thrilled to help him.

I went to his studio to meet him and his lovely wife, Bea. I modeled for him several times as he worked on his trick rider, which would take two years to complete. He also came out to watch me practice.

Spirit of the West: Celebrating the iconic 'Rodeo Series' bronzes by Lawrence Tenney Stevens

In early 1967, while I was engaged to Saddle Bronc Rider, Roy Rodewald, we went to visit Steve's work in progress. We were amazed at Steve's energy and enthusiasm as he showed us his close-to-completed statue. He had been working for two weeks on the flower for the girl's hair. Wearing a flower in your hair was a tradition of trick riders of the time. He asked us to critique the statue and the flower in progress. Of course, the statue was very impressive. However, I tactfully told him I thought the flower looked a little heavy. Steve shocked both Roy and I by saying, "That's the wonderful thing about clay," as he mushed the clay flower between his hands to start all over again. We stood there with our chins dropped to our chests. As an artist, time was nothing to him, but perfection was everything.

Girls' Trick Riding – A symbol of grace and daring, captured through the artistry of Lawrence Tenny Stevens

Femininity entered the Series with "Girls' Trick Riding," an event of spectacular daring and one of startling contrast to the tough, masculinity of the cowboys and their events.

Dazzling in their vividly-colored outfits and bewitching with their feminine grace, trick riders added an aspect to the rodeo that Steve had to capture.

When he approached Candy Coverdale, a Scottsdale gal and one of the country's top trick riders, with the idea of a statue, she was quite willing and gave freely of her time, opinion and elaborate equipment. She lent Steve her complicated $500 saddle for close-up work and gave him candid judgments on his progress.

When it came to the girl's face, Candy told Steve that the expression he had given her was no doubt good taste for sculpture, but that actually she practiced a joyful, abandoned smile while performing. This kept people from guessing if she were tired, sick or perhaps even scared at that moment and gave her an aura of absolute self-assurance.

With that tip, Steve learned one of the many secrets of the talented performers he had been watching — that of keeping an audience in a state of awe and at one with the performer in concentration. It was this same secret that Steve had unconsciously been capturing in his rodeo bronzes and that gave them the same audience appeal engendered by the actual event.

Feminine strength meets sculptural brilliance: Lawrence Tenny Stevens' inspiration for the Trick Rider statue, modeled by Candy Coverdale

The completed statues, one for each event in the rodeo, would tour the Valley National Banks in Arizona for years. Chase Bank bought out Valley National Bank and placed all the statues in a vault for many years. To my surprise, I learned that the trick rider, the bull rider, and the barrel racer were donated to The Pro Rodeo Hall of Fame and Museum of the American Cowboy in Colorado Springs last year, 2024, and are all on exhibit in the lobby.

Roy and I received a beautifully framed and signed photo of the statue as a late wedding gift.

A stunning framed and signed photo of this statue—a cherished late wedding gift for Roy and me.

CHAPTER 6
THE LOVE OF MY LIFE – ROY RODEWALD

I was eighteen when I met this handsome saddle bronc rider at the Denver Stock Show in January 1966. There was a definite mutual attraction, but I didn't get to go on a date with him until a year later. He informed me that I was too young to date the previous year. When he returned to the Denver Stock Show in 1967, I was nineteen, and he was twenty-eight.

Roy 1967 San Antonio Bronc Riding

Roy bronc riding, Ft. Smith AR 1968

Roy NFR Qualifier 1967

Roy seemed worldly to me and impressed me with stories of his adventures. He had four brothers and one sister. The three oldest brothers, Dale, Duane, and Roy, rode broncs together, while the youngest, Don, and the next youngest, Glenn, also rode broncs as a pair. Their sister, Joyce Rodewald Cattoor, was right in the middle of all these cowboys. Roy told me how they had flown to Brussels, Belgium, to ride in the World's Fair Rodeo in 1958. He said that when they left, flying over in First Class, he thought he would never see another poor day in his life. Unfortunately, the rodeo ran into financial trouble, and Gene Autry covered the cost for the rodeo participants to be flown home—but not in First Class.

I found Roy to be mature and responsible, and on top of that, he was a Christian, like me. We didn't date for long before we started talking about getting married, including some serious discussions about where we would live. I told him about how the dry heat in Scottsdale was good for my health, and he told me about the dry cold in Craig, Colorado. He was in the process of building a new house in Craig, and that was the deciding factor. I was impressed with his work ethic and prepared to follow him anywhere. I'm not sure that he ever proposed. We just started planning and came to an agreement to get married.

Roy and Duane Bros Dale 1958 Brussels

On May 15th, 1967, we were married in my hometown of Scottsdale by my brother-in-law, Anita's husband, who was a Lutheran pastor. It was a small, informal wedding with family and friends. We didn't send out invitations, but simply called people and told them to come. I wore a simple white dress, and soon after, we were headed to a rodeo in Las Vegas for a working honeymoon, where our adventure together began.

I had a 1965 Chevy half-ton, two-wheel drive, short-bed pickup. My talented new husband built what looked like an overhead camper with a ramp that folded down to the ground. That served as our horse trailer for my trick riding horse. Fortunately, saddle bronc riders don't need to bring their own horse.

We bought a sixteen-foot travel trailer to use as our residence on the road. Our new system was a bit flawed as we had to unhook the trailer to put the ramp down and let the horse in and out. It would have been more than I could handle on my own.

We arrived in Las Vegas and began our lives together in our new mini house, and soon discovered it was a bad idea not to splurge on a swamp cooler. The scalding hot weather in Las Vegas quickly taught us that.

That discomfort was multiplied by the fact that I had never cooked anything before, and this was my first attempt. My mom did not welcome me in the kitchen and I'd always far preferred being outdoors. I remembered that she would often bake potatoes, and that didn't seem too hard for me to do as a beginner. I turned the oven to 450 degrees and baked potatoes for an hour. The camper was soon sweltering at over one hundred degrees. I added humidity to the heat by cooking a few chosen food items on the burner top. The heat was nearly unbearable. Luckily, Roy was as patient as he was handsome, and he took it all in stride.

After eating, we toured the airconditioned casinos to give the camper time to cool down to 105 degrees. We didn't have enough money to eat out or gamble. We only had each other, which was new and special. Roy won some money in the bronc riding, and I got paid for trick riding, then we headed back to Scottsdale to pick up my belongings to transfer to our new home in Colorado. We also splurged on a new swamp cooler for our camp trailer. We moved my things to the almost-finished house in Craig, then began our summer rodeo circuit.

After many miles and a lot of flat tires, we realized the load we were hauling was a bit too much for my small pickup. As a temporary solution, we got split rims for our tires, which stopped us from having blowouts on our travels. We were able to buy a new three-quarter-ton truck about a year later. It handled our load much better.

We had a successful summer. Roy qualified for his first National Finals Rodeo in Saddle Bronc Riding. The top fifteen competitors in each event, based on money won that year, get to compete at the Finals. The National Finals were held in Oklahoma City, then, rather than Las Vegas as it is now. We were thrilled to go there, and it was a different experience for me as I was there as a spectator instead of performing as a contract act. It was awesome to watch the best in the business competing for the top money.

The top 15 saddle bronc riders are qualified to ride at the National Finals Rodeo. This is determined by the amount of money won throughout the year. The riders draw their horse's name out of a hat for each of the performances. Roy's most notable draw was the bucking horse of the year, Descent. Roy won money on that ride and some others, and it was a successful trip overall. And fun!

Roy on Descent Nat Finals Rodeo

While we were at the NFR, Roy's father sold the house in Craig for us. Roy and his brothers had a plan to build houses, apartments, and duplexes and sell them for profit. So, once we got back to the dry cold of Craig, Roy put the finishing touches on the house, and I moved my stuff out. We stayed in our travel trailer at a nearby trailer park for a short time until we were forced to move into an economical rental when the temperatures went below zero. Roy started building our second house between the winter rodeos.

In spite of only going through ninth grade, Roy was one of the smartest men I have ever known. He also was a hard worker. He dug the foundation for our new house by hand, then laid the cement, framed it up, roofed it, closed it in, ran the electricity, installed the plumbing, built the cupboards, laid the rocks for a beautiful stone fireplace in the living room, and finished the trim. I was constantly impressed.

I got to assist him, mainly by tracking down his misplaced tools and keeping the books. I did get to help shingle the house and paint the inside. I learned two valuable lessons. During our shingling process, I learned it was never the right temperature on the roof. It was either cold and windy, or the heat made you feel like you were in a frying pan. I also learned that one coat of paint did not mean you were done. Painting was Roy's least favorite job. When I proudly announced to Roy that I had finished the inside painting, he said, "Great! Now, do it again."

We moved in long before it was finished. I had to constantly dust and clean the sawdust off of everything, including the inside of the kitchen cupboards, as at that point, the cupboard doors were in the process of being made in the living room. Also, the white marble rock fireplace, covering an entire wall, was being cemented together.

1968 was a harder year. My father was terminally ill with pancreatic cancer, perhaps caused by a lifetime of smoking. I was twenty, and he was sixty years old. I cried all summer while traveling with my tolerant new husband. I loved my father dearly and couldn't imagine life without him. He died shortly after the Phoenix Rodeo, where I was trick riding. He waited for me to complete the rodeo before he passed in the hospital.

CHAPTER 7
LIVINGSTON, MONTANA 1968

The beauty of Montana is striking. Roy and I were in awe when we arrived in the small town of Livingston, Montana for their 4th of July rodeo.

I had a new horse named Midget. She was a little bay mare, not very tall but long-bodied like a thoroughbred racehorse, and she loved to run. She ran as fast as she could when I did tricks where she had to support weight on one side, but when I did a stand centered in the middle of her back and leaning into the wind, she literally flew.

A lot of people don't like mares, and there are some I am not too fond of, but I believe if you get a good mare, they have more heart and will give you all they have.

Midget belonged to some friends of ours in Craig, CO. They thought she would make a good trick riding horse, and their instincts were correct. When I started training her, she would watch what the other trick riding horses did and follow their pattern of circling the arena and stopping at the end. I had never had a horse do that before. Midget didn't care what you did on her—you could stand on top, drag off her side, or hang off her back end next to her flying hooves—as long as she could run, she was happy. She certainly rated at the top for my favorite trick riding horses.

Candy on Midget Liberty Stand Salinas, 1968

We had a day to relax before the start of the rodeo, so we used trick riding tape, which is basically lawn chair webbing, and made a pen extending from Midget's stall so she had room to move around and relax before the rodeo started and she had to be confined to her stall.

She was content to stay, even though she could have ducked under the tape and been free.

We were looking out the window of our travel trailer and noticed Renee Loney, my fellow trick rider's two-year-old daughter, using one of Midget's back legs as a climbing pole to get on her. Midget bent around to sniff the little girl, apparently wondering what little Renee was doing. The mare's motherly kindness was apparent, and she had no interest in harming the small child. She was just enjoying the attention. I knew, at the moment, I had a very special horse.

I had a white trick riding saddle, as many trick riders do, and it looked good on the little dark bay. To enhance the look, I made her four white leggings from six-inch wide white elastic with zippers. They were fastened on her leg just above the fetlocks and below the knees. She now had a white saddle with four white socks to complement it.

The first performance at the Livingston Rodeo was soon to be one of the most dangerous of my career as a trick rider. We flew around the arena for the first three tricks. My final trick was the liberty stand. Midget's great speed enabled me to extend my body forward over her neck. I was feeling the adrenaline of this fantastic trick when she hit the beginning of the curve in the first turn. I saw the ground coming toward me at such great speed that I didn't have time to take my hands down from their outstretched position, and at that moment, I asked God to take me as it looked like I would soon be in His arms. I hit the rocky ground face first and felt the weight of the horse rolling over the top of me. When the dust settled, my feet had come out of the straps, Midget was standing near me, and I heard the announcer saying, "Friends, this is the worst wreck we have ever seen." Roy, my husband of one year, picked me up and carried me out of the arena.

We were unable to figure out what had happened. Then, one of the observant cowboys approached us with one of Midget's white boots. It was the boot from her left front leg, which was on the inside of the turn. He handed us the ripped boot he had recovered from the arena and explained that when she hit the turn, the extension of the back leg caused her to catch her back shoe on the top of her front boot, literally jerking her lead leg out from under her and ripping the boot in half. This caused her to summersault with me standing on top of her.

I DON'T KNOW SH*T ABOUT HORSES

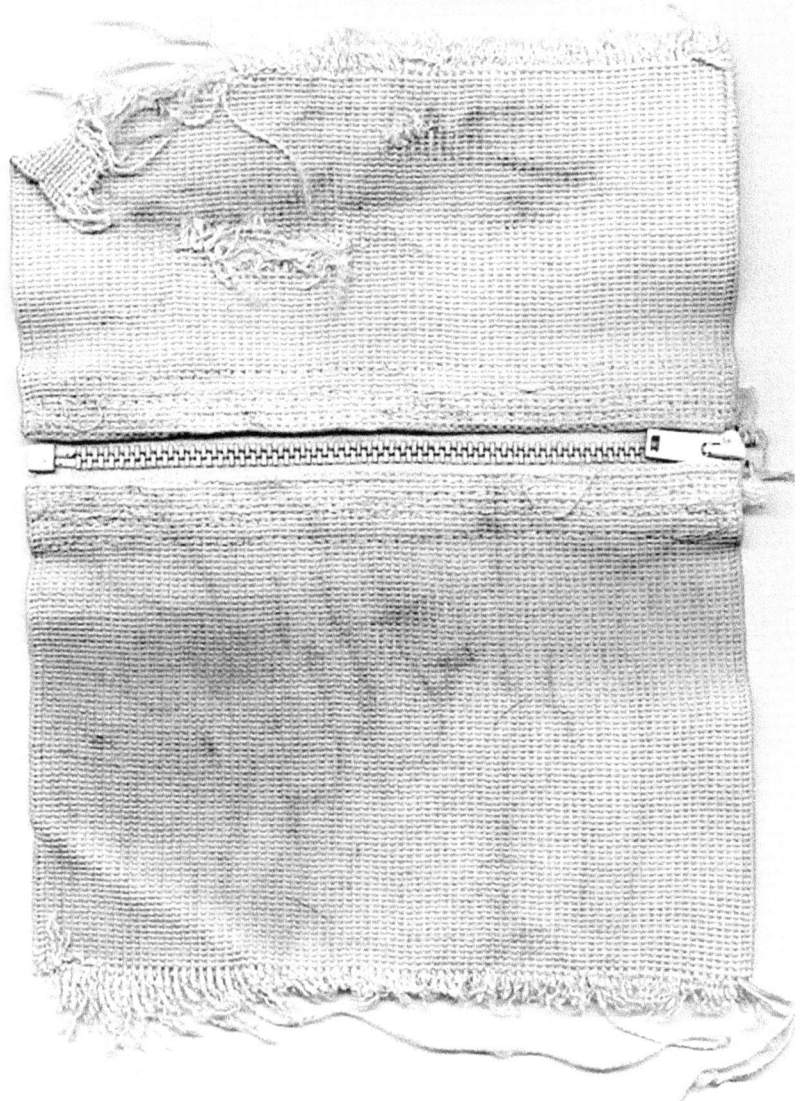

Midget's ripped white boot

It happened so fast that I did not have time to get down from my trick, which no doubt saved my life. If I had sat down in the saddle, the horn would have gone through my body, severely injuring me.

The six-inch high trick riding saddle horn held Midget high enough above me that I didn't absorb the full weight of her body coming over the top of me. However, it did bend and crack the horn. The next morning, we were off to the welding shop to get the horn repaired, as that was the first of four performances.

The show must go on!

We made it through the rest of the performances without further problems, then proceeded to our next rodeo in Joseph, Oregon, a beautiful town set in the mountains, where they were filming the movie "Paint Your Wagon."

Candy Trick Roping, Phoenix 1968

CHAPTER 8
THE COW PALACE 1968

Roy had just qualified for the 1968 National Finals Rodeo in Oklahoma City for the second time. He had tied for Champion Saddle Bronc rider at the prestigious Cow Palace Rodeo in San Francisco, CA, with Larry Mahan, who would go on to win six All-Round World Championships and eight individual championships in the rough stock events. This win gave Roy enough money to qualify in twelfth place. This was in November and the finals were in December.

I was also trick riding at the Cow Palace that year with fellow trick riders Connie Griffith, Vicki Herrera, Bill McEnaney, and Jimmy Medearis. It was a special time for Roy and I. We were on cloud nine.

Candy Cossack Drag, Cow Palace

Candy Trick Roping, 1968

I DON'T KNOW SH*T ABOUT HORSES

Roy NFR qualifier

Stroud Layout on Roxie, Preston, ID

Roy decided to learn to trick ride, reasoning that we could double the money that I made at each rodeo. With that goal in mind, we followed Connie and Dick Griffith south to Palmdale, CA so Roy could learn from the finest. Dick Griffith was a former World Champion Trick Rider in the days when it was a competitive event. He was also a five-time World Champion Bull Rider. At this point in time, trick riding was a contract act that we were paid for. Dick had taught many greats, such as his wife Connie, his son, Tad, Karen Womack-Vold, Jimmy Medearis, Kathy Crow, Vicki Herrera-Adams, Dick Hammond, and many more.

We soon arrived at their house in the desert to begin our new endeavor. Roy proved to be a quick learner, and by the third day, he was doing an outstanding job with his vaults and a trick called around the horn and vault. Circling the horse to the left, he would swing his right leg over the neck of the horse in front of the horn and follow with his body. Thus, he would be sitting in front of the horn, facing the rear of the horse. Then, he would drop his whole body off the left side, facing the front of the running horse, hit the ground with his feet, and vault back into the saddle.

The sun was setting in the west and the desert temperature had cooled. The last thing I heard Roy say was, "One more run." He turned his horse to the left to circle the arena; the horse was running very close to the fence. Roy swung his right leg over the neck, following it with his body, with his left leg extended toward the fence. His left leg swung out too far and crossed over the top of the fence rail. When it got to the fence post, which was a telephone pole, his leg wrapped around the post as the horse passed by at a full gallop. We heard the crack and the groan that came from Roy's distressed mouth.

Roy later told us he knew he had to get off as the trick horse was well-trained to not stop until he got to his station at the end of the circle.

When Roy got to the bend of the circle, he let go, sliding to the ground off the running horse. His lower leg took the form of the letter v as he landed. We were all in shock. Roy crawled forward, pulling his body with his hands to straighten his broken lower leg. Dick ran to comfort Roy, but all he could do was sob over the top of him, as he felt so bad. Connie and I were in a panic mode and crisscrossed each other at a run, screaming, "We need to call an ambulance." Meanwhile, Roy, lying in pain on the ground, was trying to organize the crazy crew who were intent on helping him but were too mentally unstable to do so.

He said, "You have a station wagon. Just load me in it and bring me to the hospital." None of us were listening. We enlisted Bonnie Happy, who was there, to call the ambulance from the house; that was long before cell phones. We waited forty minutes in the cold evening air for the ambulance to arrive. It was a long way to the hospital, but we finally arrived, the darkness mirroring our moods. In the hospital, they pulled Roy's leg out straight, and I passed out with no one to catch me.

It was an especially sad time as Roy knew he would be unable to compete in the NFR, which was just a couple of weeks away. Roy decided not to let the doctors pin his leg based on the experience of a friend of his, who'd had a similar break. His friend's leg got infected when it was pinned, and he wound up losing it to gangrene. This decision meant the healing would take longer and be more painful. They put a full cast on Roy's leg from his foot to his hip.

A few days later, with my horse loaded in the camper-like stock rack that Roy had built for her on the back of the truck, and our sixteen-foot travel trailer hooked on behind, we headed down the road, away from our dear friends in Palmdale. We had a painful six months ahead of us before Roy got his cast off.

Ft. Smith, AR 1968 on Midget

CHAPTER 9
1969 – 1973

I discovered that I was pregnant at the start of 1969. Within two weeks of learning that exciting news, my body started making things less than exciting. I had extreme morning sickness and threw up constantly. It was not a fun time.

Roy was delighted. He loved children and would have been happy to have a houseful. The pregnancy continued to be challenging right to the end, as our baby stayed inside me for almost a month past his due date. Our first child, Rhett, was born in Craig on October 1, 1969. I resumed trick riding in early 1970.

Candy, Rhett and Roy

We decided to move to Loveland so I could breathe better in the slightly warmer, dry cold weather on the eastern side of the Rocky Mountains. My asthma, which hadn't bothered me too much since I was a child, had flared up again in the extreme cold of Craig. In Loveland, Roy built two duplexes and a larger house than we had previously built.

MEXICO, HERE WE COME! Spring 1972

Roy and I happily married and with our first child, Rhett, had a grand and life-changing adventure in the spring of '72.

Humberto Craviato & Rhett, 1972 Mexico

My friend, Connie Griffith, had worked in Mexico City at a restaurant called Mission Del Campanario (Mission of the Belfry), and she'd recommended me for their entertainment job as a trick rider. It was a new venue for me, to trick ride at a restaurant, but it seemed like a fun idea, and the pay was good for steady work.

The ceiling of the restaurant was stained glass in a rounded shape at the top. It had a belfry on the outside. The elevated tables overlooked and surrounded a bullfighting arena—a perfect circle. It was small compared to the rodeo arenas I was used to, so I held each trick for two laps before changing to a new trick. I shared the venue with a talented sidesaddle riders' drill team led by 1969 Charro Completo champion Guillermo Hernandez Morones; the incredible tenor Humberto Craviotto (you can find his songs online, including his well-known album La Voz Maravillosa de México); renowned Mexican actor Carlos Auguste, who recited moving poetry while his horse side-passed gracefully across the arena; and Guadalupe Bustamante, a masterful Mexican trick roper. A talented dressage rider was also part of the program. We did two performances a day at 6:00 and 10:00 p.m., six days a week. I am so thankful for the kindness, memories, and friendship that was extended to us by everyone in Mexico.

Goodbye Party, 1972 -Mexico City

I DON'T KNOW SH*T ABOUT HORSES

Brochure where Candy trick rode in Mexico

The owner also had a unique restaurant in the nearby city of Texcoco called Cortijo La Morena (translated: He courted the Brunette). It was the same arrangement as Mission Del Campanario, except the bull ring in the middle was not covered. At this restaurant, you could also play bullfighter and try your hand at fighting the bulls before, after, or during dinner. They were not full-size, grown-up bulls, but they were pretty ornery, nonetheless. Roy got to experience bullfighting for the first time, and it worked out well with just a few bruises to show for it. Unfortunately, these two restaurants no longer exist.

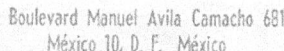

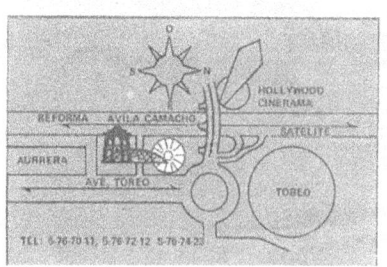

The announcer and the manager were the only ones who spoke any English, so I had the opportunity to expand the two years of limited Spanish I had gained from High School. I made big improvements in my pronunciation by exposure to the official language for a few months. I also made some progress in my vocabulary. The disadvantage now is that when I talk to someone, my accent makes them think I am much more fluent than I am. I am presently diving into daily practice on the internet site Duolingo to hopefully improve my fluency at seventy-seven years of age. I hear it helps your brain as you age, so it gives me a goal.

Back to our journey to La Capital. Sometimes, the journey to your destination is the most adventurous part of the story, and such was the case this time. We thought getting there would be the easiest part of the journey, but we were soon proven to be wrong.

We stopped for the night in Laredo, Texas, a border town to Mexico, planning to go through customs and be on our way the next morning. I had papers to allow me to work in Mexico and all the health papers for the horse.

The next morning, as planned, we crossed the USA border into Mexico. When we got to the Mexican border, we discovered there were some problems with my working papers, and I would have to return to the US to complete them for my entrance to work in Mexico.

However, since we had already crossed the USA border into Mexico, my horse could not return to the US without a seven-day quarantine in Mexico. We were able to put my black mare, Pepper, into a stall on the border and found a motel nearby in Nuevo Lardo, Mexico. It was one of the motels that had a big horseshoe driveway around a swimming pool, with parking in front of the rooms.

Echeverria was the President of Mexico at that time, and he was praised by the Mexican people for reducing the amount of violent crime they'd had there when he began office. We soon learned that Mexico had a few problems left.

The gentlemen in the room next to us were sitting out by the pool with Roy when a car drove around the pool at high speed. Roy didn't know why his newly-found amigos suddenly disappeared. They came back shortly after and explained to him that they were with law enforcement and stationed there to track down the cartels. They had feared that the car was the cartel members out to get them. There were four of them, and they were young and afraid.

We had the perfect draw to make friends with the Mexicans. That draw was Rhett, our blond-headed, two-year-old boy. The law enforcement officers beside us would bring Rhett a toy or a treat every day that we were there. Occasionally, we would walk by their open drapes and see an arsenal of guns and semiautomatic rifles on their beds. Somehow, after several days, we sorted out the paperwork and were finally on our way across the barren desert to La Capital.

My family was not in the wealthy class, but I had never experienced hunger outside of being late for dinner or skipping a meal. So, I wasn't prepared for the poverty that I would soon see in Mexico. As we drove through the desert, we would see people standing by the road, selling things. One lady selling some small animals that we thought Rhett would enjoy. We pulled over and purchased a small rodent from her. I attempted to speak with her in my limited Spanish, but I didn't understand most of what she was saying. We got back in the truck with Rhett's new pet and continued our journey. About forty-five minutes down the road, it occurred to me what the lady who sold us the critter was trying to tell me. Tears flowed down my cheeks as I realized she was telling me she was hungry. We had food in our travel trailer, and I probably would have given her most of, if not all of it. I had a new awareness of what poverty was about.

We settled our sixteen-foot travel trailer into an RV park near the restaurant, and Pepper was settled in a stall at the restaurant. We planned to stay for three months. They eat late and work late in Mexico, possibly due to the much-needed afternoon siesta, and because my shows were all in the evenings, we had all day to explore the Capital of Mexico, Mexico City. It was a pretty special time and one of the few times we got to play tourist during our travels. We visited the nearby pyramids and got to enjoy so many things and experience the culture there.

We hosted a party at the trailer park for our friends that we worked with and learned a special lesson about Mexican families. In the USA, when you invite twenty people to a party, you are lucky to get fifteen. In Mexico, when you invite twenty people, you may have forty or more show up. Those invited bring aunts, uncles, brothers, sisters, parents, kids, and grandparents. How cool is that! Anyway, it made for a great party.

As we were coming to the end of our stay in Mexico, I realized I was pregnant by probably about a month. Fortunately, I was not affected by the side effects of nausea and exhaustion to the extent I was with my first pregnancy, and I felt well enough to keep riding the final shows.

During my trick riding performance one evening, I dropped down into the tail drag, a trick where I had each foot in a strap on each side of the back of the saddle and my body hanging down over the tail of the horse with my hands dragging in the dirt. Suddenly, Pepper panicked, changing from her controlled run to a flat-out run for her life in the small circle. The centrifugal force threw me from straddling Pepper's haunches with my legs to the outside of the circle, dragging my body against the wall.

Roy was able to jump into the arena and somehow grabbed my horse by her head, hoping to stop her. She threw him off her head, but she did slow down and turned to the center of the arena, now bucking and kicking. I was thrown over the top of Pepper's back end, and one of my feet came out of its strap, leaving me hanging by one foot and tossing me under Pepper's belly. I was helpless to do anything but watch her hooves fly at my face as she kicked at her belly. At least she had stopped running.

Roy regained his footing, and two bullfighters who were dining in the restaurant jumped into the arena to help. The bullfighters grabbed Pepper by the head and were able to stop her. Roy, along with some more helpers who had joined the crowd to save my life, were able to lift me high enough to remove my foot from the strap and free me from that dangerous situation. If that accident had happened in a big arena or an open racetrack, which was where we frequently performed at home, the chances of someone rescuing me would have been remote.

This horrible accident was caused because the strap between my cinches broke and caused the tight back cinch, which is set further back on a trick riding saddle, to slip back and flank my horse. Pepper was hurting and terrified, trying to save her life. We are often at fault for our horse's misbehavior by making some unintended mistake or forgetting one thing that causes the problem. Ask me how I know…

Roy and I decided that with one young child and one on the way and only four days left in my contract, it was probably a good idea for me to retire from trick riding. After a few day's rest and a well-attended goodbye party, we headed home to Colorado.

CHAPTER 10
WINDING DOWN OUR RODEO CAREERS

We soon settled back into our American lives, traveling to rodeos and building our new home in Loveland, Colorado. Our second son, Ryan, was born on February 26th, 1973, soon after we moved out of the duplex we had been living in and into our new home.

After his six-month stint in a full cast, Roy returned to riding and even returned to the saddle broncs after a while.

Shortly after Ryan was born, Roy went to ride at the Estes Park rodeo, about thirty-six miles from where we lived. It was rare, but I stayed home that night with the kids. When Roy came home later, he looked like he had been beaten up.

He told me his story. He said he had been bucked off over the head of the horse with both feet still in the stirrups. Unable to free himself, the horse ran over him, kicking him as he did so. Fortunately, his feet came out of the stirrups before he was drug too far, and he survived without any serious injuries. I was worried and sympathetic but thankful he hadn't been killed or hurt worse than he was. I encouraged him to rest that night.

Over the next few weeks, and after many conversations, Roy decided he had a bigger responsibility to stay in one piece to raise his two boys, so he chose to switch from bronc riding to team roping.

Roy took up team roping, that's what old bronc riders do. And I took up barrel racing, that's what old trick riders do. We loved our horses and would continue to enjoy them, but the time had come to change our plan.

Rhett, Ryan and pony

Roy, Rhett, Ryan and Candy

Roy had always dreamed of flying, and he now set out to fulfill that dream. He took lessons in Loveland, got his license, and purchased a small, four-seater, high-wing Cessna 172 airplane. We made many exciting trips west over the Rocky Mountains to visit his family in Craig, Colorado. I did not get as much joy out of flying as Roy. Every time we crossed the mountains, the wind currents would push the plane up, then drop it down many feet, and motion sickness would often overtake me, and I'd end up throwing up. On one trip, we headed south to Arizona. It was a really rough flight, and we ended up landing in New Mexico. When we landed, the boys and I climbed out of the plane, and Ryan, our youngest son, and I stood under the wing, and both threw up. I wasn't sure if he'd ever want to fly again. I was wrong.

Roy with his Cessna 172, Rhett in plane

Ryan, who had experienced his first horse wreck in my belly and definitely had the 'thrill-seeker' genes on both sides, turned out to be our adrenalin junkie. He rode bulls, trick rode, rode saddle broncs, and learned to fly airplanes. He is now an airplane pilot for Jet Blue Airlines out of Orlando, Florida. He has plenty of stories to write in his own book. Hopefully, that will happen someday. Ryan and his wife Kelli have two boys. Their oldest boy, Riley, was the only one that Roy got to have some fun with before he passed. That was a special blessing for him.

Ryan on Smoky Jo Calgary 1994

Ryan on Smoky Jo high crupper - Calgary

Our oldest son, Rhett, did a lot of building with his dad as he grew up and wound up building two houses in the Colorado Springs area with his wife, Shelly. He went on to be a computer programmer. He and Shelly had four grandchildren for us—three girls and one boy. Unfortunately, they all arrived after Roy passed away and he didn't get to see them. He loved children, so that was sad.

Our grandkids with Danny, the pony

We had purchased a seven-acre property from Dick Hammond in Colorado Springs not long after we were married. I had trick ridden with Dick before he went into the real estate business. We decided to move from Loveland to Colorado Springs so our boys could go to Redeemer Lutheran School in Colorado Springs. So, off we went to start a new adventure in our lives together.

Construction Colorado Springs House

Candy, Roy, Ryan and Rhett – Colorado Springs house

Trick roping with boys & Fred

Roy and Candy Rodewald

Smoky Jo and Candy Reining Slide

Ryan bronc riding

Ryan bronc riding like his dad

Change Your Plan

When I was team roping with Roy, I took a Team Roping Healing Clinic from World Champion healer Walt Woodward. In team roping, there's a chute in the middle where the steer is kept. The header is on the left side, and the healer is on the right side in a boxed area. Walt told us, "When you back your horse into the box, you've got to have a plan."

One roper said, "I have a plan, but I'm not roping very well." Walt's reply was simple but profound: "Change your plan."

At the time, I didn't think much about it beyond the context of team roping, but as I've grown older, I've found myself applying that advice to many areas of my life. Sometimes, changing the plan is exactly what you need.

When Roy and I lived in Colorado, I loved the state's beauty but never fully enjoyed the cold weather. Over the years, as I aged, the winters became harder to tolerate. In 2023, I finally took Walt's advice and decided it was time for a change. After more than 50 years in Colorado, I sold my two businesses and moved to Florida. The Lord guided me every step of the way.

Selling my businesses was no small task, but it felt like the right time. I sold Sunset Stables to someone who had boarded horses there, and I sold my storage business without even needing a realtor. The Lord brought buyers to me, and I reinvested in the company with Crystal View Capital out of Las Vegas, who now manages it wonderfully. My house also sold quickly to a kind young couple, and before I knew it, I was packing up my things, letting go of what I no longer needed, and heading for a fresh start. I arrived in Florida in March 2023 and bought my house in April.

The change was freeing. Florida's warm weather and abundant activities have been such a blessing. I've even joined the Morning Star Cowboy Church here, where I continue to feel the Lord's presence in my life.

But changing plans hasn't always been easy. I still wrestle with my love for riding. My childhood idol, Roy Rogers, once said, "When you're young and fall off a horse, you may break something. When you're my age, you splatter." That quote has stayed with me. As much as I'm tempted to ride again, my body doesn't enjoy it the way it used to.

Through it all, I've leaned on the Lord for guidance. I praise Him for every experience—the good and the bad—because I've learned so much with Him by my side. Life has been full of changes, and I'm thankful for the wisdom to know when to change the plan.

As I look forward, I'm excited for the day when I'll see my loved ones who have gone before me and spend eternity with the Lord, where there will be no more pain or suffering. Amen.

CHAPTER 11
A TRIBUTE TO MY SPECIAL FRIEND, CONNIE GRIFFITH

Connie Griffith was a dear friend and fellow trick rider. She was fifty-five years old when she performed 'Under the Belly' at the National Finals Rodeo, which was an amazing feat for a woman at any age. Not many trick riders, male or female, last that long, and the ones that do rarely do such dangerous tricks as this one, which involved sliding down the side of the horse, reaching for a strap under the belly, and going under the belly of the running horse and up the other side.

Connie Griffith 1970s

Connie would say there would never be a time she would not trick ride. Ironically, a short time later, she was killed in a freak trick riding accident in St George, Utah. She was there with some students, performing at the rodeo. She was sitting on the neck of the horse in front of the six-inch metal horn facing the rear of the horse, when her horse, Winnie, tripped in a barrel hole going around the top of the circle pattern and did a forward roll over the top of her. The weight of the horse and saddle crushed her body as it rolled over her.

The hospital called me that night, wanting to know if I had her mother's phone number as she would not make it through the night. I was able to help them with that information. My heart was broken.

We were blessed to have Connie, Dick, and their son, Tad, at our house in Colorado Springs for a visit. We would sit around the kitchen table and tell stories and literally laugh until we cried.

My beloved friend, Connie, always said she was collecting stories for a book. Unfortunately, she never got that done. She said, "No one would believe them anyway." With the help of her son, Tad, we put together a couple of her stories as a tribute to her. I am hoping Tad writes a book containing many more stories of their adventures. Here are two of those stories.

Connie Griffith Story #1: Over the Mountain

Having just finished their Trick riding performances at Ouray and Ridgeway, Colorado, Connie, Tad and the rest of their group left with two rigs headed back to Scottsdale, AZ. Tad said his mom would look at the map and select the road that was the shortest distance to their destination. However, she never bothered to look at the legend on the map.

Tad said, "I learned that when I look at a road on a map, and the road is very squiggly and goes over a mountain, it is not really a shortcut, especially if it is grey. A grey, dotted line is a goat trail."

Tad believed that this was his mom's most famous shortcut. It turned out to be a logging road with many switchbacks. To make it more exciting, the truck Connie was driving had a failing transmission and bad brakes.

Connie's Aunt Belva, who was in her eighties, was keeping her company in the truck as they proceeded up the steep Colorado mountain. When the transmission could no longer do its job, Connie was at a standstill on the hill.

Tad was in the truck, following close behind her. It was being driven by a fellow trick rider as Tad didn't yet have a license to drive. He jumped out of the truck to let her know they were going to push her until they could find a shoulder to get off the road and out of the way of the logging trucks. He said she had her window rolled down, probably to keep her awake as she was tired. Connie could not see their truck behind her. Tad ran up beside her, but before she saw him and he could explain what they were going to do, Aunt Belva jumped out of the truck and began to try to push the truck with the door open.

Connie was amazed at her aunt's determination and bravery. She was even more amazed when the truck began to move forward up the hill with her aunt pushing it. As they began to move, Belva jumped back into the truck, thinking she had done her job. Without their knowledge, the other truck had caught up and was pushing from behind. Tad was laughing so hard he couldn't talk.

When Connie was called about working at a rodeo that summer, she did not discuss how much they would pay her but instead asked about the elevation she would have to go over to get there. Tad said they worked a lot of flat country rodeos that year. It was hard to make enough money to pay for the repairs their truck needed. Their solution, when they got to a mountain, was to unload the horses and ride them over the mountain in the bar ditch, then load them again to continue their journey. They usually had enough help with them to both ride the horses and drive the truck.

At one of the rodeo dances, Connie was chatting with some friends. They said, "We thought we saw you earlier this summer, but it couldn't have been you because they were riding their horses over the mountain pass."

Connie replied, "Yes, that was us."

Tad was in the background, embarrassed, and thinking, "Mom, they didn't know. You didn't have to tell them it was us."

Tad told us that when they were at Thompson Falls, Montana, at Dick Vincent Ranch Rodeo, his parents decided to leave before the rodeo was over for the first time in Tad's life. Because of the complications they were enduring traveling, they thought it would be a good idea so they could make it to their next rodeo in time. They usually would leave the following day. This time they loaded up and began to drive out the only road, just before the bull riding event started, the final event of the rodeo. They made it to the one and only exit over a cattleguard, and they got stuck on the cattle guard, unable to move forward.

By then, the rodeo was finishing, and many people wanted to go through the gate they were blocking. The waiting line was rapidly growing. They unloaded the horses and pushed the rig over the cattle guard and off the road, then watched as everyone who had watched them perform passed by them and waved. Miraculously, after everyone went by, they were able to start the truck, reload their horses, and be on their way.

Connie said, "The rodeos were incidental; the trips were the memorable parts."

Tad thought it would have been a good idea to put a tong on the truck so they could hook up the horses to pull the truck. They never actually got that done.

Connie Griffith 1967 doing Ted Elder Drag

Connie Griffith Story #2: Road Block

Connie, Tad, and Dick had a new situation. They had consolidated the many rigs they had been driving into a single-axel semi-truck, pulling a very heavy bull trailer. Dick was not physically able to drive any longer, and Connie, at minus five feet, was unable to reach the pedals on the semi-truck. Tad did not yet have a driver's license, let alone a semi-truck license, so when Connie informed him that he would be the one driving the truck to their shows back east, he was shocked and told her, "I have never driven a semi-truck." She quickly arranged a practice drive before they left the small town of Wickenburg, AZ, with a skilled truck driver they had hired to drive the truck on one of their first trips with it.

He must have done very well on their long drive to North Carolina, as there were no exciting stories. I am sharing with you what happened on their return trip to Arizona.

They were on Interstate 40 going through Tennessee. Tad was pretty sure because the highway patrol hats were similar to cowboy hats. Tad was driving and his mom was in the sleeper. In the distance, Tad spotted the flashing lights of patrol cars that were detouring trucks off the road to the long, downhill off-ramp. He said to his mom, "You must drive."

He slowed to about 35 mph on the long downhill ramp and traded places with Connie—a feat only two trick riders could do. He was now positioned in the sleeper with his head right behind her where he could talk to her and give her instructions on how to drive the truck. Connie had a driver's license but not a truck driver's license, so I am not sure what the legal benefits would have been.

Tad instructed her to step on the brakes to slow the truck down. Air pressure brakes on a semi take longer to begin stopping than hydraulic brakes on a pickup truck, so, discouraged that she was not getting the expected immediate result, she released the brakes, and they picked up more speed going down the hill. On the second try, even though Tad was instructing her to keep her foot on the brake, she instinctively did the same thing. Part of the problem was that Connie's short legs were unable to put enough pressure on the brakes.

On the third try, Tad said, "Mom, you have to keep the pressure on the brakes to stop the truck."

Connie basically slid off the seat, using the front of the seat for a backrest so her short legs could put enough pressure on the break to eventually bring the truck to a screeching halt, but not before the two Highway Patrol officers, one on each side, who were flagging the truck to stop, had to jump out of the way into the ditch, to avoid being hit. The horses in the back were dancing about, trying to keep their balance but were able to reorganize themselves when the truck came to a stop. Luckily, they were packed tightly enough together that none of them fell.

Tad was in the sleeper with his hands over his face, saying to himself, "We are all going to jail." He had good reasons for his thoughts. Here they were in a single-axel Mac, pulling a big cattle trailer with no insurance, no mud flaps, missing clearance lights, no truck driver's license, bald tires, and almost running over two Highway Patrol officers. On top of that, they had other riders in the front of the truck with them, making them two people over the legal limit to be in the truck cab. The officers regained their footing and walked back to the truck, scratching their heads, trying to figure out what had just happened. They were shocked to find petite Connie at the wheel.

Connie, the eternal optimist, was smiling and trying to converse with them. They didn't seem to be interested in talking and continued their inspection, walking around the rig. Much to Tad's amazement, they both raised their arms and, pointing with their fingers, signaled them to continue their journey. Tad could only imagine what they were looking for. Maybe drug traffickers or a semi-load of bodies?

Now, the journey back up the steep hill began. Tad was now reaching down, trying to put the truck in low gear while telling his mom not to give it any fuel but just let the clutch out slowly without stepping on the gas. Her pickup truck instincts kicked in again, and she stepped on the gas, causing the truck to bolt forward. The horses were scrambling for their footing once again. She did this twice more, causing much jerking and stirring of horses. When she finally put the clutch all the way in, the truck slid back to the start between the two men who had jumped out of their way upon their arrival. They were wondering how they could have made it that far and were now unable to leave.

Now, with a clearer understanding of what Tad was telling her, Connie slowly let the clutch out in low gear, and the truck proceeded up the hill at about two miles an hour. Tad was okay with the slower speed as it was a tremendous improvement over the jerking and going backwards.

Halfway up the hill, with about fifteen trucks slowing following them, they again traded places. Tad took the wheel, and they headed for home.

Roy and Candy enjoying life

CHAPTER 12

BAD NEWS BOB, THE REDNECK SCHNAUZER— ALSO KNOWN AS BIBLICAL BOB

I received Trinket, a four-and-a-half pound, long-haired Chihuahua, as a gift from friends in our bible study when my beloved husband of thirty-four years passed away in 2001. Her love and vulnerability helped me summon my strength and gave me a soft body to hug and soft fur to cry in. Though she was tiny, she came with an attitude, and I figured she needed a friend.

Trinket

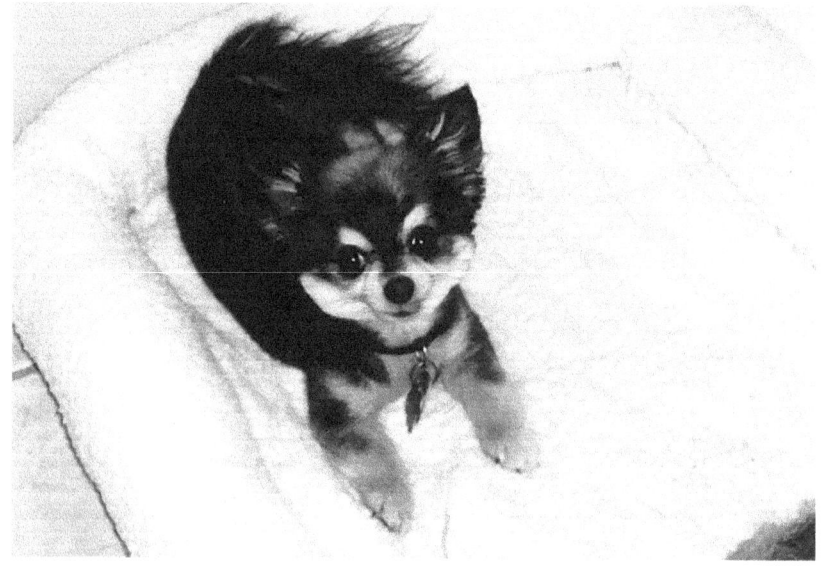

Trinket

The breeder that Trinket came from sent me a picture of a miniature schnauzer puppy. He was irresistible, so of course, I rushed to get him.

My daughter-in-law, Shelly, a veterinarian, had an idea that we should call him Bobble, as in Trinket and Bobble. So, Bobble it was. However, it soon became apparent that the name was not a very good fit for the roughneck little Schnauzer, so we shortened it to Bob.

I didn't send Bob to the groomer for an official Schnauzer cut, so he was a little rough looking. My friend, Cheryl Harper, proclaimed that he was a redneck Schnauzer. Bob's adventurous ways endeared him to all. His name soon was lengthened to Bad News Bob, the Redneck Schnauzer, or Bob for short.

When it was time to neuter Bob, Shelly put him on her table to begin the procedure. A sniff of gas to put him to sleep was all it took, and he was dead. Can you imagine what it would feel like to have your mother-in-law's dog dead on your operating table? Shelly swung into action, giving him mouth-to-snout resuscitation. After ten minutes of hard work, Shelly felt life coming back into the little dog's body.

We later learned that Bob had an extreme allergy to anesthesia. He had a sibling that died on the operating table, and that veterinarian had assumed it was an overdose.

Bob soon came home, but due to the long time without oxygen and the damage done to his brain, he was unable to stand, walk, hear, or see. Because of his young age, Shelly thought he would regain those functions.

Poor little Bob! I would wash him in the sink each morning as he was unable to stand, even to go potty. After several weeks, he began to relearn how to walk. He would scramble to his feet, then tumble into a forward roll. It would have been funny if it hadn't been so pathetic. Soon, he was up and going again but would run into things, as he still did not see. We could not call him, as he still was unable to hear. Bob recovered his senses, one by one, and after a few months, he was enjoying life again.

Bob

Bob enjoyed following my horse, Snert, on trial rides through the desert when we went to Arizona to escape the cold of the Colorado winter. I had convinced Roy, years earlier, that spending a month or two in Arizona each winter was a good idea. When Roy finally conceded, he said, "The birds with their tiny little brains are smart enough to fly south for the winter, so why not us." I continued to head south in the winter after he passed.

Bad News Bob would cover at least twice the miles that my horse did, as he would crisscross back and forth, exploring everything. Bob's schnauzertude would often get him in trouble. On one ride, I had to speed Snert up to get between Bob and some coyotes he planned to take out.

Going forward three years, I sold the seven acres and house in Colorado Springs, where we had lived for close to thirty years, and moved to Pueblo, CO. The acreage was sold to a developer who had no need for the house. He was kind enough to allow me to salvage whatever I could out of the house, so with our two sons' help, Bob, Trinket, and I were back in the Springs, taking windows, garage doors, cupboards, and whatever we could salvage.

While we were busy disassembling the house, Bob followed his nose and wandered off. He always found his way back, but this time he failed to return. After a long search, I headed back home to Pueblo, heartbroken. That evening, I received a call from a lady who had picked Bob up and brought him home with her. I called Ryan and Kelli, my daughter-in-law, who lived near the Colorado Springs house, and they went to retrieve Bob. She opened the door but said she had let the dogs out, and Bob had disappeared again. Ryan and Kelli drove the neighborhood, calling Bob's name, when a gentleman called to them and asked if they had lost a little dog. Bob was soon back in my arms.

Thus, the nickname Biblical Bob. He was dead, and he is alive; he was blind, and he sees; he was deaf, and he hears; he was lame, and he walked; he was lost, and he was found. His story covers the whole book. Amen!

Bob's next miracle happened in Arizona a few years later. He was playing with some big dogs, and one of them playfully thumped Bob on the head with his paw. The next morning, when I opened the door of my living quarters horse trailer to let him out, he just stood at the door, shaking. It soon occurred to me that he could not see. I brought Bob to Terri Gold's Vet Clinic. She diagnosed detached retinas with no hope of ever seeing again.

I bought Harley (my other small dog at that time) a bell for his collar so Bob could follow him. To my delight, three days later, Bob's sight was back, and he was following the horse on the desert trails again. I inquired of my daughter-in-law, Shelly, if the vet might have made a mistaken diagnosis, and she informed me that it was pretty straightforward and easy to diagnose a detached retina. It was unlikely a mistake had been made. So, that was Biblical Bob's second miraculous recovery from blindness.

Praise the Lord!

NBHA World Championships Senior Finals 2011

CANDY COVERDALE RODEWALD

By Susan Gentry
Photos By: Kenneth Springer

Candy Rodewald, NBHA Senior 2D World Champion tells Cowgirls In Style magazine that she didn't start barrel racing until she was in her 40's.

Her love for horses started with her heroes, Roy Rogers and Dale Evans. She became a trick rider by the time she was 14 years old. The widow of bronc rider Roy Rodewald, Candy has 2 sons and 6 grandchildren. She is living a life that most would only dream of.

WITH AN ENTHUSIASM FOR LIFE, CANDY RODEWALD HAS BEEN A TRICK RIDER FROM THE TENDER AGE OF 14 TO WINNING THE NBHA 2D WORLD CHAMPIONSHIP AT 64

With her many interests and accomplishments that have been a big part of her life., Candy is a humble, personable woman with a love for life.

We invite you to enjoy our interview with Candy Rodewald.

Q's & A's with Candy Rodewald

Cowgirls In Style **Where are you from?**
Candy: Born in Chicago, IL moved to WI at 3 yrs by 7 I had asthma so bad the Doctors told my parents I needed to move to AZ. I started 2nd grade in AZ and grew up there. In 1967, I married handsome bronc rider, Roy Rodewald who moved me to Colorado. I have been there ever since, now residing in Pueblo.

CIS: **Tell a little about yourself:**
C.R. I live in Pueblo CO in town and am able to have my horses at my house. I am close enough to the Arkansas river to be able to enjoy trail riding beside it. There is a small arena with 2 round pens right by my house owned by a neighbor who is generous enough to let everyone use it.

I DON'T KNOW SH*T ABOUT HORSES

CIS: How did you get started with horses?
C.R.: My heroes were Roy Rogers and Dale Evans. It seems I was born with a passion for horses. My parents were not horse people, however when they saw there wasn't anything they could do to stop me they were supportive. In Arizona we lived down the street from a stable. I would do anything to get a chance to ride. Clean stalls, horses, harnesses, whatever. I graduated to being the ride wrangler early on. I became a professional trick rider by the time I was 14 yrs old. My mother would make beautiful costumes and my dad would drive me to rodeos.

CIS: How and when did you start barrel racing?
C.R.: I didn't start barrel racing until I was in my 40s. The boys were older and I had more time to ride. My neighbor, Dixie Pring, was supportive and helped me get started barrel racing.

CIS: Other events in your life you have done and are currently doing?
C.R.: I love to dance and help people and grand kids with their horse skills. I have enjoyed and competed in, to one degree or another, team roping (healer) Dressage, reining, jumping, trail riding, horse showing, trick riding and trick roping.

Candy competing in the 2011 NBHA Semi-Finals in Georgia

CIS: What competitions have you won
C.R.: In 2011 I won the Open 1D in Wickenburg, AZ Racing in the Rockies winter series. NBHA Senior 1D for the State of Colorado. NBHA Open 1D for my Colorado district. NBHA Senoir 2D World Championship at the NBHA world show in Perry, GA. In 2009 and 2010 I won the 60 yrs plus Southwestern regional Championship in the Senior Professional Rodeo Association. My horse Snert has won 7 saddles and numerous buckles for me. He has been a blessing.

CIS: What is your fashion style?
C.R.: Jeans and boots

CIS: What are your goals?
C.R.: To be able to ride and learn for the rest of my life.

CIS: Any tips you would like to give?
C.R.: The basics are the basics are the basics... learn them, teach them to your horse and you will excell in any disipline you do. Work hard, perservere and be greatful.. Learn all you can from everyone you can, every horse you can, every clinic and book in every discipline you can, and continue doing so for a lifetime. You won't ever learn it all.

Candy trick riding Fort Smith, AR in 1965 or 1966.

CIS: Tell us about your family?
C.R: I was married to bronc rider Roy Rodewald for 34 years untill his passing in 2001. We have 2 fine boys Rhett and Ryan and I have been blessed with 2 wonderful daughter in laws and 6 grandchildren

It has been an honor and a pleasure to have featured Candy as our "Around the Barrel" spotlight.

Know of someone who you think should be featured in our "Around the Barrel?"
Please contact us at:
info@cowgirlsinstyle.com

Cowgirls In Style Magazine Interview

CHAPTER 13
2013—SOMETHING I DID THAT WAS BAD

This still bothers me today. You know how sometimes you think you have done something good, but learn you have done something very bad? This was one of those times.

I was riding my horse in the arena by my house in Pueblo. A young lady, who had been hanging around and watching me help others, approached me. She said she wanted to ride and asked if I would be willing to teach her. She was in her early teens and a big girl for her age, and her mannerisms reminded me of me at that age. She appeared shy and hesitant to ask a favor of anyone. I could no longer charge money, as I had dropped my liability insurance due to the high cost, and now only taught people that I wanted to. I really liked her and said I would be willing to teach her if she would be willing to help me with the horses. I was scheduled to get a new hip in two weeks and would need some help with feeding.

For the first session, she brought a relative—a cousin, I believe. So, instead of one student, I had two.

She must have decided she was imposing by bringing an extra student, so she came alone the next time. This time, things went well. She rode in the round pen on my horse, Snert, and we worked on her balance. It is important to have your balance on a horse. Otherwise, you are balancing on his mouth through the reins, which is uncomfortable for the horse. One of the best ways to learn this is on a lunge line in an English saddle.

The lunge line is a long rope attached to the bridle, with a person in the center who guides the horse to circle around her and take his cues from voice commands. This way, the rider can work on her balance without worrying about where the horse would go or needing to give aids. The rider starts out holding onto the saddle with the inside hand in front and the hand on the outside of the circle holding onto the back of the saddle. When the rider can feel her seat move with the horse and stay balanced, the rider first lets go with one hand, and then the other. As they become comfortable doing that at each gate—walk, trot, and canter—other exercises are added. One is to stretch both arms out to the side, then reach over their head, then to the front.

I, personally, did not do these exercises until I was in my forties after being a professional trick rider and doing many other horse activities, and I was amazed by the confidence they gave me. The lesson went well, and she helped me with some chores.

I believe it was about the third lesson when things went wrong. I was a little anxious about the upcoming operation on my hip in about a week. I knew she had a lot to learn, and I started pushing her hard. Too hard. Since she was going to help me with chores while I was recovering, I felt she needed to learn to work with the horses on the ground.

Horses are herd animals. In the herd, one horse is the leader or boss, and then each horse in that herd follows an order of dominance, from the most dominant to the bottom of the pecking order. The order does not always stay the same and positions may switch from time to time. When we enter the corral, the last one in line looks at us and says, "Finally, I don't have to be last anymore."

To establish our dominance, we need to use the same techniques that horses use with one another. If you observe them, they will ask the other horse to move his front end away or to move his back end away. They may do that by moving their head, pinning their ears, sometimes baring their teeth, or turning their butt toward the other horse in varying degrees of aggression. We have to remember that most horses weigh from 800 to 1,200 pounds, which makes us pale in comparison. Horses will respond to our requests depending on where their head is that day and how they perceive our request. If they are sensitive or spooky, it will take very little to ask them to yield to us and a gentler request would be in order. If the horse is dominant or lazy, you may have to be more aggressive.

First, I demonstrated the different ways we could use to ask the horse to move. We can twirl the end of a long lead rope, bringing it closer to them and increasing the speed as we get nearer, and in some cases, letting the end come in contact with the horse. This must be done with intention and rhythm, not by just throwing the rope at the horse. Often, people will twirl the rope at the horse but their body will step away. The horse immediately senses your fear. You can also hold both hands in the air, flicking them toward the horse's neck and nostrils as you walk toward them in a half circle, asking them to yield to you. This can work well on a more sensitive horse.

As my student began to work on some of these things, her quiet mannerisms and shyness did not impress Snert, and I was concerned for her safety. So, I aimed my demonstrations toward her. I asked her to move away from me by coming aggressively toward her with my hands up and flicking. She did move away because she could see I was serious. I also demonstrated how to use the flat of the hand against the horse's shoulder to ask him to move by applying my hand in a slapping motion to her hip. She had been trying to use her weight to push the horse out of her way, which was nearly impossible. My demonstration seemed to help her understand what I meant, and she finally made progress, but we had a long way to go. We then saddled the horse and worked on her riding; I felt it went well.

That evening, I called to ask her about something. Her father answered the phone and started yelling at me.

"How can you call yourself a teacher?" he yelled. He said I had traumatized his daughter and even hit her. He went on and on. He told me she would not be back.

I was in shock, not realizing the severity of my actions. I wrote a note to them, saying that my intention was not to hurt her but to keep her safe, but I neither heard from nor saw them again.

That was many years ago and there is rarely a day I don't think of her and regret that I hurt such a delicate flower. I guess I need to learn to read people as well as I read horses, and I would be a better teacher. I wish I could tell her that, sometimes, when you care for someone, you are tougher on them than if you just don't care.

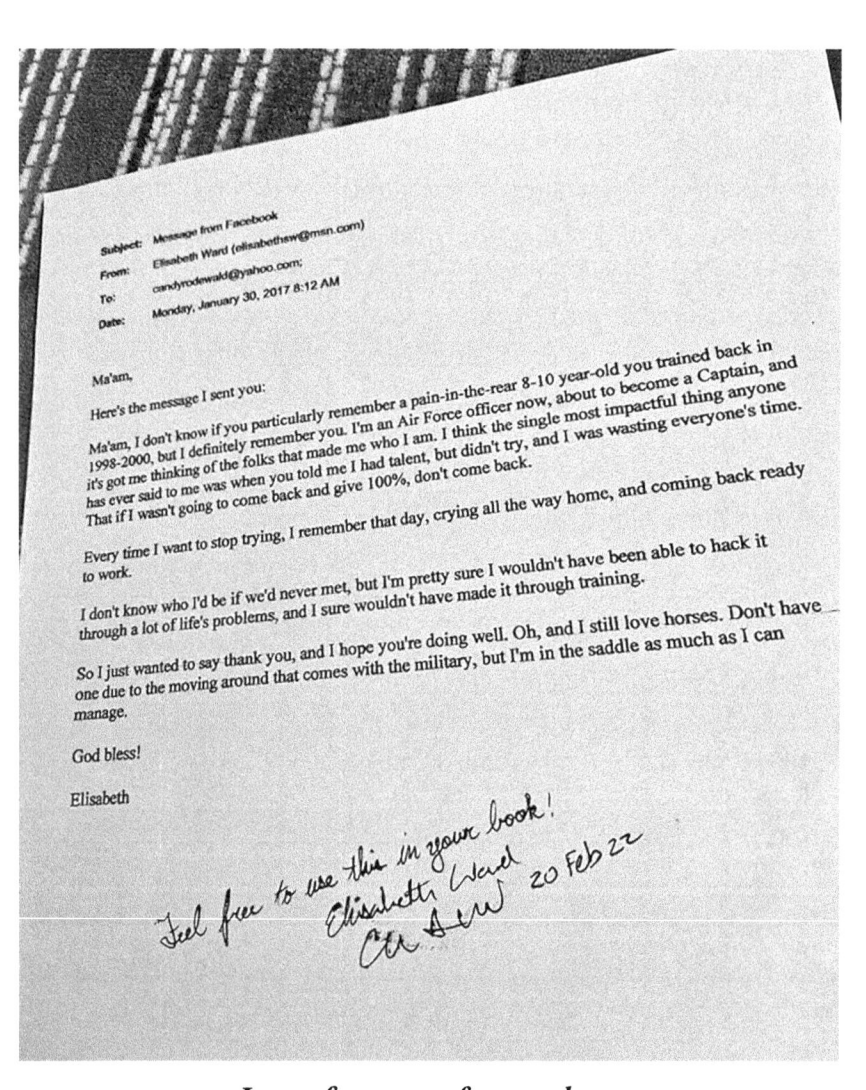

Letter from one of my students

CHAPTER 14
PONY CART WRECK #1—JANUARY 2013

Roy went to be with his Lord in 2001, but I continued to head south in the winter whenever possible. I arrived in Arizona on the last Sunday in January of 2013 with my three-horse, with living quarters, trailer in tow, carrying two horses—Snert and Sassy—and a cob pony named Posh. I'd had a hip replacement done at the end of November, so I was anxious to get back to my horse activities. I longed to enjoy the warm desert on horseback, but with my recent hip operation, I was cautious and decided to play it safe by hooking up the pony cart and going for a drive.

Posh was a beautiful bay pony I had acquired through a friend. He was a former rescue pony and had his share of issues. I had been driving him for a year and a half and he was doing very well. However, he was having a problem with the bulkiness of his cart bridle. He was always trying to rub it off his head. Having compassion for his problem, I decided to change bridles for my first cart ride in Arizona.

I hitched him up to the cart, and my friend, Ed, had ahold of the bridle as I climbed in the cart, reins in hand. I announced, "I've got him," and Ed let go and turned around.

At that moment, Posh reared up and took off like a 747 taking off down the runway. Observers told me he was running so fast the wheels could not keep up and were making a rut in the dirt. Dave was driving his four-wheeler toward his trailer; I shouted for him to watch out and luckily missed hitting him.

We continued at a dead run to the pens where the other horses were. I was thinking in slow motion, "He just wants to get to his friends. Surely, he will stop when he gets to the horse pens." Wrong!!!

He ran straight toward the pens, and before he ran through them, he made a sharp right turn with no reduction in speed. The pony cart flipped on its right side, and I went flying in a twelve-foot arc in the air. As I came down head first, I tried to catch myself with my outstretched left arm. The force of the speed and motion turned my elbow completely backward. That might have helped break the fall a little as I landed on a rock with my cheek and left eye.

With the cart dragging on its side, Posh panicked even more and continued to run. He circled the pens and the outside of the roping arena at least three times before he ran into the desert, clipping the back of a moving tractor as he went.

I heard him running past me, and I was desperately trying to get up when Bonnie, who owned the ranch, came and held me down, fearing I might further injure myself. I was trying to reason with her, saying we were both going to be run over, but she was not listening to me. Meanwhile, I was thinking that if I'd wrecked my new hip, the surgeon who did the operation was going to kill me. Posh was still running when the fire truck and ambulance arrived.

Posh didn't stop running until he had ripped the harness so badly that the cart came unfastened and dropped to the ground. Sadly, the ordeal left Posh badly injured. He was unable to lower his head to eat, and he was clearly in great pain.

I was hauled first to one hospital, then to another—Good Samaritan in Phoenix, specializing in trauma care. I had spent much time there as a child dealing with my asthma. I was four days in the hospital before they found a doctor who could mend my elbow.

Dr. Scott Edwards, an Orthopedic Surgeon, walked into my room. He was young and good-looking. That took me by surprise, as all doctors used to be ancient. I guess I was now the ancient one. His confident personality spoke to me, and I will never forget his words when we first met. He said, "Candy, not many people can fix this, but I can."

The relief on my face must have been evident. "You do it," I said.

Dr. Edwards had been a surgeon in the military and had no doubt seen many injuries that would make mine pale by comparison. He explained that he would put in four pins to reconnect the various broken bones. He warned me that I may not be able to fully straighten my arm after the surgery.

After a four-hour surgery, I was wheeled back to my room. Dr. Edwards visited me and instructed me to not ride my horse for six weeks because if I reinjured the elbow, he might not be able to fix it. I was not very happy, as I had trailered two horses to Arizona to ride the beautiful desert trails. I started physical therapy three times a week for two months.

Two weeks later, I had my follow-up visit at Dr. Edward's office. I did not say a word of protest about my instructions; however, I must have looked pretty pathetic as the doctor's further instructions were, "You can ride. Just don't fall off."

Thanks to this gifted doctor, my arm is completely normal. I can straighten it fully, and I have no pain in my skillfully repaired elbow. I am still grateful to him to this day. Thanks, Dr. Edwards.

In the hospital, I had plenty of time to figure out what I had done to cause this accident. I had been driving ponies since I was a child and had always used a driving bridle. By focusing on the comfort of Posh, I had completely forgotten that the blinkers on the driving bridle serve a purpose—they keep the pony from seeing the cart behind him. The English bridle, though more comfortable for him, did not have the blinkers on it. Posh had never seen that cart behind him and thought it was chasing him, thus his state of panic. As one friend used to remind me, "Every good deed has its consequences." This certainly applied here, as Posh lost his life, and I came close to losing mine. In the end, I did lose an eye.

The next week, I had to go to another hospital, where surgery was done to repair my crushed cheekbone and replace my damaged eye with a piece of coral.

After my hospital stay and a layover with my sister, Anita, who nursed me back to health, I returned to my trailer at the Privit Ranch. My friends, who had witnessed the wreck, told me that if I had died, they would have put my last words on the tombstone, which were…

"Whoa, you son of a bitch!"

October 2015, Albuquerque, NM—Balloon Ride

The sport of ballooning is not for those who like to sleep in. The balloon is prepared for its journey into the blue long before daybreak.

It was a beautiful October day in Albuquerque, NM at the Albuquerque International Balloon Fest. This is noted to be the largest balloon festival in the world. That year, they had five hundred fifty balloons in the air at one time.

Tammy and Lu Toxvard, the daughter and son-in-law of my friend, Ed Carlson, are balloonists who flew a balloon they called the Pepsi balloon. It was the colors of a Pepsi can—red, white, and blue. I was blessed to be invited on my second ride in their beautiful balloon.

After a beautiful ride, we made a somewhat rough landing with the balloon tipping sideways. Lu, the pilot, said, "Whoa, you son of a bitch," then exclaimed, "It doesn't work on balloons, either."

CHAPTER 15
REINVENTING MYSELF

Although I had spent most of my life riding rodeos and Western style, I had dabbled a bit with jumping as a child, and once my rodeo career ended, I tried my hand at other disciplines. I found a great hunter/jumper trainer, Frances Nix, in Colorado Springs, and with her help, I was able to compete successfully in several shows.

I was led into dressage training through an abused horse who needed more than I could offer. Dressage is a basic style of riding that teaches you how to use your body to influence your horse. I ended up working for many years with Pat Long, a talented dressage instructor, and I learned so much from her. I wish I had begun this training at an early age, as it is truly the foundation of riding. Under the guidance of these wonderful teachers, I have continued to learn and improve my horsemanship well into my senior years. There is always something more to learn where horses… and people… are concerned.

I was having a discussion with Frances Nix, who had become a special friend by then, concerning the changes our bodies go through as we get older. Our reactions are slower, and we are not as strong as we were, not to mention our balance. Once again, she offered some advice. She said, "Candy, as we get older, we have to reinvent ourselves." So, always open to her excellent advice, I got myself a Miniature Horse.

Picture of trick riders helping at the trick riding school put on by Karen Vold and Linda Schultz in Colorado L to R: Ryan Rodewald, Linda Schultz, Karen Vold, Dick Hammond and Candy Rodewald.

I helped with it for many years and really miss doing that since I have moved to Florida.

Candy at Duanes Ranch

December 2019—Waco the Miniature Horse (from Waco's perspective)

Hi, I'm Waco. I am a Miniature Horse. I am sometimes mistaken for a pony because I'm so small, but I am a horse in a miniature body. I measure about thirty-eight inches from the ground to my withers (a spot where the top of my back and the bottom of my mane meet). I am the smallest of all the horse breeds… and the cutest.

Up until a few months ago, I was a feral (wild) horse, and a stallion. I wandered the hills of Texas with my herd of mares. It was a hard existence; food was sometimes scarce, and being a prey animal, I had to protect myself and my herd from predators, particularly coyotes. When we were threatened by a predator, the lead mare had the responsibility of leading the herd to safety, and I would follow behind and make sure everyone followed her. If necessary, I would fight off the predator. It was hard and sometimes scary, but I was free.

One day, a pack of predators of a different type attacked my herd. They only had two legs and were all straddling a bigger version of me. Several of them surrounded me and my herd and drove us into a small, enclosed area with high fences we couldn't get through or jump over. We were trapped. I was so afraid, I didn't know what to do.

The next thing I knew, I was in a place with other feral horses, big and small. The two-legged predators captured me using a rope and took away my manly parts that made me the leader of my little herd. I didn't know what was happening, but the pain was fierce, and the noise and confusion terrified me. So far, these creatures had caused me and my family only fear and pain. There was no one to trust, and we were all very afraid.

We were forced into a large, dark box, which moved under our feet and terrified us even more. When we were finally allowed out of the box, we were in a place called Colorado, at a 'rescue center.' There were many other horses there that had come from different places. Some had been starved and abused; some were wild, some were old, and some looked pretty healthy. All of them were confused, frightened, and unwanted, like me.

I learned that predators with two legs were called humans. One day, a human called Susan brought me and one of my mares to her home. Susan called my mare Spinner, as her fear caused her to spin in rapid circles. She named me Chump.

I didn't trust Susan at all, so she had to rope me to catch me, but she was gentle and patient and spoke to me in a kind voice. I was afraid, but I didn't want to hurt her. Food was plentiful and I enjoyed that. She taught me about going forward from the pressure on the halter and how to step up into one of those big boxes, called a horse trailer. One day, after she had worked with me for about two hours, she quietly slipped on my back. Her feet were only four inches from the ground on either side. I had never felt anything like that, but I was tired, so I tolerated the new weight on my back.

Then, the weather turned really cold for about two weeks, and I didn't get worked so hard.

One day, another human named Candy showed up. She played with me in the round pen, and I could tell she thought I was adorable. Susan told her about sitting on me, and once again, she walked me around and then slipped on my back. This time, I had more energy because of my long rest and short workout. She felt like a mountain lion on my back, and I bucked to see if I could get her off. It wasn't long before Susan was picking herself up off the ground. The good news is she didn't have a long drop to the ground and was not hurt.

Soon, Susan was loading me into another box. They shut the gate, and I was headed, all by myself, to a new adventure with Candy.

When we arrived at Candy's, I was unloaded, and we walked down a steep hill to where there were two other horses. It felt like I was in the hills of Texas again, and my new adventure began.

"Work hard, persevere, and be grateful. Learn all you can from everyone you can, every horse you can, every clinic, and every book in every discipline you can. Continue doing so for a lifetime—you won't ever learn it all. And if you think you know everything, you are probably wrong."

-Candy Rodewald

CHAPTER 16
ON THE ROAD AGAIN WITH ELEVEN ANGELS

After seventy-two years of life, I still hadn't gotten used to the cold after growing up in Arizona. I was also having a hard time adjusting to what I wanted to do versus what my body was capable of doing.

I had been driving a large heavy camper pulling a horse trailer behind it, an experiment that is now over. I didn't like the struggle of driving it, especially when the wind tended to blow it sideways. I was informed by my son that it was too dangerous for me to drive. Without the help of my husband, it became far more challenging to do the physical work involved in driving "on the road" again. We'd had a camper in the '90s and pulled a horse trailer, which worked out well. But even then, I lacked the strength and skills to do what he did with it. Among other things, I have had to hire someone to put the camper on and off the truck.

After selling my camper, I was undecided about what to do. Then, I saw a very nice used 2008 DD three-horse trailer with living quarters on the internet and purchased it.

Siblings Candy, Anita, Bill and Nancy

I made a quick trip from my home in Pueblo, CO, to Arizona to pick it up with the help of my friend, Ed. I had a visit with my sister and cousin while we were there, and then we returned home to enjoy Christmas before I headed to Florida to visit my son and family. That trailer would supply me with my fair share of adventure in the coming months.

To start, the new trailer came with two large plastic containers filled with liquid that I thought the former owner had identified as gasoline. I asked my two strong grandsons, who were visiting during the holidays, to take the heavy five-gallon cans out of the side of the trailer and put the gasoline in my little Ford Escort, which they happily did.

Later, I jumped into my faithful little '98 Escort with 250,000 miles on it to drive the short distance to my business. I had driven less than a mile when the engine choked and quit in the middle of the road. At least four cars stopped to push my car off the road to the safety of an Economy Mini Storage parking lot. The kindness of those strangers renewed my faith in humanity and gave me a preview of the angels to come on my up-and-coming trip to Florida.

I had the Escort towed to the auto shop, where the problem was identified as water, not gas, in the gas tank. It turned out to be a blessing in disguise, as my little car ran better than ever after it was fixed.

But it was about six days before I planned to leave for my Florida trip that my real saga began. I had put some eggs to boil on the top burner in the house, then mentally ran through all the things I still needed to do before leaving. I decided to turn off the burner while I ran some errands. It was a great idea! However, when I returned three hours later and opened my door, smoke poured out of the house. In my rush, I had forgotten to turn off the burner on the stove. I worked many hours cleaning up the mess and trying to get rid of the smoke smell.

When I finished cleaning, I went to the basement to get the mop, which was in the furnace room. I stopped in shock at the sight of water covering the floor. I immediately called the heating company, and upon examining it, they announced that they would have to replace everything in my hot water heating system, including the water heater. It would take about four days, during which I would have no hot water or heat. The good news was that they would provide space heaters to keep the house warm. Not being one to want to miss my daily hot shower, I gave them a key, bid them goodbye, loaded Snert and Waco in the trailer, then hopped into my truck with little Chico, my rescued Chiweenie, and headed south.

It was already afternoon by the time I left, so I knew I wouldn't make it far, but I thought it would be worth getting a good start. My first planned stop was Clayton, New Mexico. It was dark before I pulled into a truck stop in Clayton to find that, unfortunately, all their parking spaces were full. Due to my lack of night vision, I didn't want to go any further, so I pulled across the street and parked on a wide shoulder near a residential neighborhood. I didn't unload the horses but fed them and proceeded to get them fresh water from my large plastic tank on top of the trailer. I pulled the hose out to fill the buckets when the connection, hose and all, broke off, spilling twenty-five gallons of water onto the street. I filled the buckets with water from my shower and delivered them to the horses.

Chico and I cuddled up on the couch, turned up the heat, and slept. Well, kind of! The horses were restless, and every time they would move or paw, Chico would bark. As I prepared to leave in the morning, I saw a sign in front of the truck that stated, "No overnight Parking." Thank goodness we weren't fined or towed off.

At daybreak, we were on our way again. I stopped at a truck stop that morning to let the horses out and walk them around. I took Snert, my sixteen-hand barrel racer, out and tied him to the trailer, then went back to get Waco, the mini. To my surprise, Waco had escaped his enclosure in the trailer and was standing about fifteen feet away as trucks slowly went by in the parking lot. I envisioned spending the day in this small Texas town chasing down Waco, who had been running wild across the Texas rangeland only a couple of months ago. I still frequently had to rope him to catch him, and my roping wasn't that great. Although he did not have a mean bone in his body, he was fearful of many things.

He stood there, paralyzed, as the semis continued passing by. He allowed me to approach him and put my hand on his halter. He had no lead rope, and I was afraid I would lose him if I tried to lead him by the halter. By this time, the truck line was at a standstill. I asked one of the drivers if he would hold him while I got his lead rope. He kindly obliged, and Waco was soon tied to the trailer beside his friend, Snert. This was help from angel #1.

Senior 1D Colorado State Champion- Candy & Snert

Before our next stop for the night in Oklahoma, I filled the truck with diesel fuel, overflowing my tank. We stopped where the horses could have a pen, and I had an electric hook-up. The horses enjoyed their freedom, and Chico and I had a quieter night.

We were on the road again first thing in the morning. It wasn't long before I noticed my fuel gauge wasn't showing a full tank, even though I had filled it the night before. Tricking myself into believing the gauge was malfunctioning, I continued to drive on.

My truck started acting strange, and I pulled off to the side of the freeway to figure out what to do next. I decided I had a major problem and envisioned having to stay there for a week with my horses (which always complicated any given traveling problem) while my truck was repaired. While waiting for a tow truck to arrive, I had more time to think through the possibilities. The thought occurred to me that perhaps the gauge wasn't wrong, and I could have just run out of fuel. So, I called the tow truck driver and asked if he would bring some diesel. He arrived with five gallons of diesel, which he had to siphon into the tank. He started the truck and followed me to the next service station, where I filled up and made sure all was going right before he said goodbye. Angel #2

My third day on the road turned out to be the most challenging. Just northwest of Birmingham, Alabama, I pulled into a small, crowded truck stop, in need of some Blue DEF (the new liquid that makes truck emissions less harmful to the atmosphere). I decided to top off my fuel tank, even though it was pretty full, and I was careful to make sure it was full. Yes, I did learn a lesson from the previous day.

I squeezed past the vehicles to make a left at the end of the pump. I had no excuse for what happened next. Poor judgment, too crowded, I was tired… Gooseneck trailers don't follow you like bumper-pull trailers do. They cut the corners, which is why you see semis go wide to make the corners. When I made the turn to get in front of the gas pump, I caught the back side of my trailer on the guard that protects the pump. At least I wasn't the first to make that mistake, and they were prepared with padding on their guard. I tried to straighten out by backing up and then pulling forward again. It didn't work; I could not get it to move. I needed a truck driver to get me out of the situation.

I proceeded to fill my gas tank when the gentleman on the other side of the pump kindly asked me, "Do you need some help?"

I respond with the question, "Are you a truck driver?"

He said, "No, but I own a trucking company."

"Yes, thank you. I could use some help," I said.

He got in the truck and tried to back it up with no luck, so we decided a lift was needed to move the trailer over. I was envisioning the cost in my mind. Then, he changed his mind and decided to unhook it and then hook it with the truck at a different angle. With the help of his two strong sons, he was able to do that. He got back in the truck, thinking we had solved the problem, but he still could not move the trailer.

After further investigation, they discovered that the trailer breakaway switch wire that puts the brakes on the trailer in case of an emergency, had broken. As a result, the trailer brakes were on and working well since the truck could not move in either direction. While my helpers were trying to reconnect the wire unsuccessfully, a man on the other side of the pump said, "Do you need some help?"

They told him the problem, and he said he worked on wiring problems. A quick cell phone call for instructions and he was able to fix it immediately. The men also filled my truck with two heavy gallons of Blue DEF. Thanking them profusely for their kindness and thanking

God for sending them, I waved goodbye to four more angels and headed to Birmingham. Angels #3, 4, 5, and 6.

My exit was eighteen miles east of Birmingham, and it was almost the end of the day. By the time I got to Birmingham, there was only a little light left in the sky. They were doing a lot of construction on the interstate, and I sensed I had taken a wrong turn. So, I exited into downtown Birmingham. I Googled on my cell phone and asked for directions back to the freeway. It happily responded, then proceeded to send me around the same block four times. It was obviously time to change my plan, so I pulled my rig off by what looked like a factory parking lot.

I got out of my truck and ran across the street, waving down a car that was driving out of the lot. The driver rolled down her window, and as I explained my situation, I quickly realized that I was blessed to have run into yet another helpful Southern person.

"They have really messed things up with the construction," she said. "Let me see if I can figure out how to explain to you how to get on the freeway." Upon giving it some thought, she said, "Why don't you just follow me."

I hopped in my truck and followed her for fifteen minutes, making many turns before arriving at an on-ramp to the freeway. There is no way I could have followed those instructions if she had given them to me verbally. I praised the Lord for yet another angel. Angel #7

It was pitch black by now and I had eighteen freeway miles to go to my exit to the horse motel, plus another seven miles off the road. I was mostly concerned about the seven miles of narrow roads once I got off the freeway and the lack of turn-around space on those little roads in the dark should I get lost. So, I called the horse motel for instructions. The kind person on the phone told me to call again when I exited the freeway, and they would have someone drive down to meet me and lead me to the motel. He did exactly that, and I gave thanks for the blessing of yet another angel. Angel #8

The next day, my route took me to Akin, Georgia, to visit a special lady—Pat Long, my dressage teacher from Colorado Springs, who had moved to the lower altitude of Akin because of her husband's health problems.

When I was about fifteen miles from her house, I called to get more detailed directions. We were chatting and trying to figure out my location. It was complicated by the fact that she spoke in street names, and I only knew the route numbers. It made little difference because my phone suddenly went dead and did an automatic factory reset, rendering it unusable for two days.

Fortunately, I had her address written down on a piece of paper, so I drove through downtown Akin, as it was again getting dark, and businesses were shutting down for the day. I took about ten parking places and parked my rig in front of an antique store. Two ladies, who were sisters-in-law, greeted me. When I told them my situation and showed them the address, one of the women told me that she lived near there and would get in her car and lead me there. So, I was able to follow her to my friend's house. How many angels can a person have in a week? Angels #9 and 10.

I enjoyed a two-day visit with my teacher and her husband. I told him about my first lesson with Pat. I had a new horse that had been severely abused, and I knew I did not have the skills to help him, so I sought out help. I soon found out that I needed more help than the horse did. My first instructions from Pat were to ride a circle with him. When I had finished and rode back to her, she commented, "I can't believe you barrel race when you can't even ride a decent circle."

That started a three-year relationship which included private lessons with her every week. After the lessons, I would go into the house, physically and emotionally drained, and just stare at the wall. My learning experience helped me in all the riding disciplines I participated in throughout my life, including barrel racing. I often wondered why I couldn't have had her as a teacher in my early years as it sure would have made for an easier life for me and my horses.

After a great visit, I waved goodbye to my friends, looking forward to my last day on the road before reaching my son, Ryan's house in Florida. True to form, I missed a turn on the road and wound up taking every back road I could find in South Carolina, and quite a few in Florida before I reached the main highway in Florida. Once again, it was dark as I approached my destination. I missed the turn into Ryan's driveway and immediately knew it.

Almost instantly, I received a call from Ryan, who was in another state. His son, Reid, had called him, telling him that he just saw me drive by. Ryan gave me instructions, which involved driving in a circle until I came back to the road to their house, where I was to wait for Reid to meet me and drive my rig back to their driveway. Reid expertly turned into their drive and around the many trees that surround it. My last angel out of the eleven who helped me on my trip to Florida was my own grandson. Angel #11.

Oh No! Pony Cart Wreck #2

Summer 2023

I attend the Morning Star Cowboy Church here in Central Florida. You can bring your pets, which many people love—one lady even brings her parrot.

They have a program that enables handicapped people to enjoy the thrill of riding and caring for horses. This program meets twice a month. They also hold a special event once a year at nearby Lake Yale, offering participants a variety of horse activities to enjoy.

One of those activities is a pony cart ride. The Pastor asked if I would be willing to drive a pony cart for the event. Of course, I was more than happy to be part of this special program.

I got in the cart to warm up the pony. As we circled, I could feel he wasn't happy, especially when we went a little too far from his horse friends at the trailer. Suddenly, he came to a halt. I gently urged him to move forward, but instead, he stopped and backed up. His hooves slipped on the muddy ground, and he lost his balance. Then, to my surprise, he reared over backward and landed on his back, tipping the pony cart onto its side. If he hadn't slipped, he might have run forward instead—I don't know.

Fortunately, I was able to jump out of the cart before it hit the ground and did not suffer any injuries. Even more of a blessing, I was the only one in the cart. I called for others to come help. They arrived quickly and held the pony down while others unhooked him from his harness and the cart. Once freed, they helped him back up. He was not injured either.

We never figured out what caused the accident, but I am thankful the results weren't worse.

My son, Ryan, firmly told me, and I quote, "No more pony cart rides for you."

So, I changed my plans and crossed pony carts off my list.

CHAPTER 17

THE BASICS OF RIDING AS RELATED TO MY FAITH

Life can be difficult. So can riding horses. There are ups and downs, victories and defeats, gains and losses, and we will all leave our lives with plenty to learn.

1. 1. Eyes: When we ride, we must guide our horse by looking softly, not staring in the direction we want him to go. When we need to change our direction, we turn our heads, not lean with our bodies, to look in the new direction of travel. If we lean with our body and put more weight on the side we want him to turn into, we will be giving him contradictory signals. If I lean right, I will be pushing him to the left with my weight, and I will not be in a very good position to keep my balance, especially if he

is an athlete and turns quickly to the left. We look to where we want to go, and the rest will follow.

In life, we can't let difficult times keep us from looking to our Lord for guidance. We must keep our eyes on the Lord, softly, and allow him to keep us balanced. If we look for ways to bless others and don't concentrate on ourselves, we will experience the joy of the Lord.

2. Breathing: When we are riding our horse and fail to breathe, our body stiffens, and our horse, being a prey animal, feels that he has a predator on his back and will become fearful of us. His instincts of self-preservation will kick in, and he is more likely to buck, spook, or run away. If we are fearful or angry, we will pass this emotion onto our horse.

When we are fearful or nervous in life, we tend to take shallow breaths or hold our breath instead of taking a deep breath and putting our faith in God. If we can be aware of our body stiffening because of fear or anger, and take a deep breath before it progresses, we will have a better chance of calmly looking to our Lord for guidance.

3. Centering: When riding our horse, we must keep our body weight centered over the center of our horse in the middle of his back. If not, we will lose our balance and possibly end up on the ground.

We must make our Lord the center of our lives and not lose our balance and fall away from Him or be misguided by the world we live in.

4. Building Blocks: Picture you are on a horse and a crane lifts you straight in the air and sets you on your feet. Would you be able to stand in balance? Or would you be leaning your upper body back with your feet in front of you, making it impossible to stand? Think of dropping a plum line from your ear through your hip through your ankle, or stacking blocks on top of each other so they don't fall over. In this position, when the crane sets you down, you will not fall because you are in a balanced position.

    Sometimes, we lose our balance in life and in our relationship with God, too. To keep our lives balanced, we must love God and our families, work hard, and bless others.

5. Grounding: Stand in your stirrups and allow your weight to sink down into your heels. If you are pushing yourself up with your toes like a ballet dancer, you are losing connection with your horse. It is important to stay grounded while riding so we don't lose that connection.

    We must also be grounded in our Lord. By being grateful for all that you have been given in life and giving thanks to the Lord, you maintain your connection with Him.

Credit to Sally Swift and her book *Centered Riding*

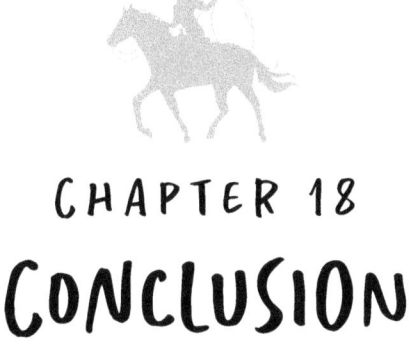

CHAPTER 18
CONCLUSION

Putting My Insights into the Basics

I taught basic riding for many years, and I am still blessed to help people, even though my body cannot do what it used to do on a horse. One of my favorite sayings is:

If you want to learn, teach. Keep an open mind because you will never learn it all in any subject.

We are blessed to be a blessing.

The basics of both trick riding and everyday riding can be taught on an artificial horse, even a barrel with a saddle strapped to it. It is easier on the horses to start that way, and safer for you.

The basics are the basics are the basics... learn them, teach them to your horse, and you will excel in any discipline you do. Work hard, persevere, and be grateful. Learn all you can from everyone you can, every horse you can, every clinic and book in every discipline you can, and continue doing so for a lifetime. You won't ever learn it all.

A SIMPLIFIED HISTORY OF TRICK RIDING

Competitive Trick Riding developed in the United States in the early 1900s. It was based on the wartime riding strategies of Cossack soldiers and adopted by American cowboys as a rodeo competition.

In competitions, each trick is awarded a point value based on the difficulty of the trick. Plus, or minus points are given for various elements of the trick. For example:

- The speed of your horse.
- How long you do the trick through the pattern. Tricks can be done on a straight-away (on a racetrack or a long arena not suited to a circle) or a circle pattern (in an arena). If you stopped doing the trick halfway through the pattern, the consequences would be a big deduction off your score. In the case of Under the Belly or Under the Neck, which are high-point tricks due to their difficulty levels and done very quickly, you would need to fill in the extra space in your pattern with vaults around the horn or other maneuvers. You couldn't have a spot where you were doing nothing.
- Was your form good? For example, on a Liberty Stand, you should not bend your knees and look at the ground.

Instead, straighten them up and acknowledge the audience with a smile.
- You remembered to sell the trick by acknowledging the audience for the last one or two strides of the trick.
- The appearance of your costume and your horse.

In the 1950s, trick riding became a paid act in the rodeos. Paid acts were referred to as contract acts. There were usually three to five trick riders in an act, each doing different tricks. Salinas, CA Rodeo was the exception, as they would have as many as ten riders performing on their racetrack between the grandstand and the rodeo arena.

In the 1960s, barrel racing and team roping were added as official rodeo events. The money needed for those events left less money for the contract acts. So, many of the rodeos that had contracted trick riders could no longer afford it. The clowns, who are also a contract act, developed acts to fill in between the events. Their main job was to protect the bull riders and having them perform extra acts cost the rodeo less than hiring a group of trick riders. It soon became difficult to make a living trick riding. I was delighted to see trick riding return to more rodeos and events in the last fifteen years with many excellent, quality performers. I am writing this October 2024.

In the early 2000s, Tad Griffith brought back some trick riding competitions, and I was privileged to be one of the judges to work with him on many of them. I think these competitions brought the skill to many new riders who'd had little exposure to it.

Served as judge in the trick riding-my photo used on poster

Celebrating the legacy of the Rodewald Family—honored for their lasting contributions to the sport of Pro Rodeo.

SCORING SHEET

Ground Work/ Performance Tricks	pt value		Description of tricks and saddle
Double vaults	18	must do 4	A trick riding saddle has a 6" horn so you can grip it with both hands enabling you to vault from side to side.
Crupper vaults pp 97 & 98	23		At the back of the saddle are two handholds called cruppers. You jump behind the saddle and use these cruppers to hold onto, to vault off the back of the horse and back on.
Ted Elder Drag page 112	37		To perform the Ted Elder drag, grasp the strap attached to the D-rings on the back of the saddle. Then, execute a forward roll off the saddle, ending up face-up behind the horse with your feet dragging on the ground. In this position, your head will be between the horse's legs, obstructing your view of both where you are going and where you have been.

Under the Belly page 108	40		With a foot in the stirrup, you step off one side and swing your body so you can get your foot in the stirrup on the other side, while also grabbing a strap on the other side and remounting the horse on the opposite side.
Slick Saddle Stand	27		You grab the horn and jump into a standing position in the saddle. You have to absorb the motion of the horse with your knees bent to keep your balance.
Shoulder Stand	28		Grab the latigo on each side, or on one side with the horn. Jump into the saddle with your knees, shoulder in front of the saddle on the horse's neck, and push yourself into a headstand, balancing on the neck.

Full Fender page 19 & cover pic	20		Start to dismount on the left side. Bring your stirrup out so you can tuck your knee under the fender. Twist your body away from the horse so you are facing the audience. I did it with my leg extended, looking up. Others bring their free leg under the the horse's belly and reach for the ground with their hands.
Strap Tricks			
Hippodrome Stand (also known as Liberty Stand or Roman Stand) pp. 19, 40 & 68	18		You have a two-inch strap attached across the front of the saddle to the D-ring on each side; the strap lays in back of the horn. You place a foot on each side of the strap, with your right hand on the horn. You use your left hand to steer the horse to begin the run. You then pull up to a standing position, using the mane with your left hand and the right hand on the horn. At the end of the run, you reach down and push on the horn, bringing your feet out of the strap, and sit in the saddle.

Cossak Drag/Russian Drag or Death Drag page 31	16		You have a sturdy strap attached to the right side of your horse, to the cinch buckle that attaches to the latigo. You adjust that strap so your knee is either in the middle of the saddle or on the left side. You twist your body to face the crowd and drop down, extending your left leg as far as you can bend it away from the horse, hopefully dragging your hands on the ground, at least on the corner.
Stroud Lay Out page 33	22		You have another strap attached to the D-ring on the right side of the horse. You put your right foot in it, with your left foot in the stirrup. Your leg should be able to extend so it is in a place where you look like you are standing sideways on the horse. This trick takes a lot of core strength.

Back Bend pp. 20 & 30	28		You put your feet in the Hippodrome strap and your right hand is on the horn. After turning your horse to go, your left hand reaches over your head and grabs the left crupper. Then, you follow with your right hand grabbing the right crupper and push into a backbend.
Tail Drag page 40 bottom of page	18		You have a strap on each side of the horse attached to the back D-rings - the ones the back cinch is attached to. You put a foot in each strap, and when you are running, you push yourself in back of the saddle, straddle the horse's hips, holding on to the cruppers, then let go and drop down with your hands close to the ground.

Judging Criteria	points		
Speed of horse	1 to 35		
Technical difficulty	1 to 40		
Execution of core trick	1 to 10		
Presentation of trick	1 to 10		
Bonus for combination	1 to 5		
Negative points for form breaks	-1 to -5	unlimited	

RODEO PERFORMERS I PERFORMED WITH

Trick Riders I Worked With	(Continued) Trick Riders I Worked With
Vicky Herrera-Adams	Connie Griffith
Karen Atterbery	Donna Hall
Bev and Oscar Berger	Dick Hammond
May Boss	Larry Lewis
Sally Boyce	Joanne McEnaney
Anita Marie Caskoski	Bill McEnaney
Brad and Sheila Frank	Jimmy Medearis
Tad Griffith	Butch Morgan
Bev Hammond	Vernon Nicholes
Edith Happy	Jill Noel
Shirley Loney- Butterfield	Jeanette Plunkett- Bolling
Linda Cassidy	Eddie Smart
Danny Craighead	Mary Stetler
Cathy Crow	J.W. Stoker
Sparky Dent	Karen Womack-Vold
Jerrie Duce	Marlene Waber
Joy Duce	Donene Whale

Trick Riding Groups I Rode With
Arena Athenans
Fire Balls
Flying Cimmarons
Star Flyers

Trick Ropers I Rode For as Horse Catcher or Roped With
Jr Eskew
Gene McLaughlin
Monti Montana
Monti Montana Jr.
J.W. Stoker
Larry Lewis

Rodeo Clowns Who Performed at the Same Rodeos
Wilber Plaugher
Jimmie Schumacher
Wick Peth
Chuck Hensen
Bunkie Booger
Wilie McCray

Other Acts Who Performed in the Same Rodeo as Me
Glenn Randel
Jay Sisler dog act
Elaine Kramer Roman Rider
Omaha NB 1966 at Aksarben
I trick rode and Roy #96 was a bronc rider

Life should not be a journey to the grave with the intention of arriving safely in a pretty and well-preserved body, but rather to skid in broadside in a cloud of smoke, thoroughly used up, totally worn out, and loudly proclaiming, 'Wow! What a Ride!

-Hunter S. Thompson

LIFE STORY TIME LINE

1947	Harry Truman predicted budget surplus Stanford University isolated polio virus. Average cost of a car $1290.00 Average cost of a house $6650.00 Gas cost 0.15 cents/gallon Average income $2,854 Cold war begins	Candy Born June 20th 1947 Chicago IL
1949	Communists control China Korean War Military integrated Berlin Airlift	Oldest sister Nancy married
1955	Little Rock AR Martin Luther King	Brother Bill went to law school in Berkley We moved to Arizona from Wisconsin I started 2nd grade in Scottsdale
1963	JFK assassinated	Feb - Trick Rode: Scottsdale, AZ. My 1st RCA Pro rodeo

	Civil Rights March on Washington	June - Santa Maria, CA
		July – Salinas, CA
		August - Payson, AZ
1964	Beatles	Junior in High School
		February – Trick rode, Chandler, AZ
	War on Poverty	March - Imperial, CA
		April - Springville, CA and Red Bluff, CA
		June - Santa Maria, CA and Camp Pendleton, CA
		LA Coliseum
		July - Prescott, AZ and Salinas, CA #2
		Santa Barbara, CA Hemet, CA
		Sept - St George, UT
		IRA ASU INTER COLLEGIATE RODEO
1965	Operation Rolling Thunder Vietnam	Graduated from Scottsdale High School
		February - Trick rode Scottsdale, AZ, Yuma, AZ
	Watts Riots and the Montgomery March	March – Imperial, CA
		May - San Jose, CA and Ft Smith, AR Missed HS graduation to get to Ft Smith on time

		June – Gallup, NM
July - Meeker, CO, Nephi, UT, Salinas, CA #3, and Ogden, UT
August - Burwell, NB, Lawton, OK, and Payson, AZ
Fall - purchased truck new 1965 Chevy half-ton pickup $2,100
1966	June 13 Miranda established N.O.W. formed	May - Jasper, TX, Kansas City, MO, and Ft Smith, AR
July - Livingston, MT, Butte MT, Calgary, AB, Canada (hit deer on way) and Salinas, CA #4
August - Phillipsburg, KS, Burwell, NB, Chehalis, Centralia, WA
September - McAlllister OK and Omaha, NB
October - Raliegh, NC, Got to see prejudice up close in the South

| 1967 | Peace movement / Detroit riot | January – Trick rode Denver, CO
Started dating Roy Rodewald
Roy qualified for the National Finals Rodeo
May: Married Roy Rodewald May 15th
Las Vegas, NV honeymoon
May-June - Ft Smith, AR
July - North Platte, NB, Mobridge, ND, Kalispell, MT and Salinas, CA #5
August - McAllister, OK
September - St George, UT
October - Montreal, Quebec and Winnipeg, MB, Canada
In December 1967, Roy qualified for the first time as one of the top 15 saddle bronc riders and competed at the National Finals Rodeo in Oklahoma City (now held in Las Vegas). It was a great year for us both. |
|---|---|---|

1968		March - Phoenix, AZ and Indian trade fair
	Martin Luther King murdered	May-June - Ft Smith, AR, Vernon, TX, and Mandan, ND
	Robert Kennedy murdered	July – Livingston, MT (had wreck), Butte, MT, Polson, MT, Salinas, CA #6, and Joseph, OR (another wreck)
		August - Preston, ID and Bremerton, WA
		September - Ellensburg, WA and Pendelton, OR
		Oct-Nov – San Francisco, CA, Cow Palace
		Roy again qualified for the National Finals Rodeo in 1968 in Oklahoma City. Tragedy struck when he broke his lower leg in half while learning how to trick ride two weeks before the finals and was unable to compete that year.
1969	First man on the moon	1st son, Rhett, born in Craig, CO 10/1/69
	Richard Nixon inaugurated	

1970	Massacre at Kent State	March – Trick rode Phoenix, AZ and Indian Rodeo
	EPA established	July - St Paul, OR, Salinas, CA #7, Ogden, UT, and Evergreen, CO
		August - Colorado Springs, CO
		September - Bremerton, WA and Ellensburg, WA
1972	Nixon re-elected	February – Tucson, AZ
	Watergate Scandal	May - Trick rode Mexico City June to July 4th Trick rode
		June to July 4th – Trick rode at Mission Del Campanario in Mexico. Had career ending accident
1973	US withdraws from Vietnam	2nd son, Ryan, born in Loveland, CO 2/26/73
	Nixon impeached	
1974	Nixon resigns	Worked at House of Neighborly Service
1975	Vietnam falls	1974-75-76 with Georgia Thompson
		Candy volunteered at Unicorn Crisis Line

1976	Jimmy Carter elected President July 31 - Big Thompson Flood – Estes Park to Loveland – 135 people died	Moved to Colorado Springs from Loveland Ryan (kindergarten) and Rhett (grade 2) attend Redeemer Lutheran School Friends were in The Canyon the night of the big Thompson River Flood We moved a week or two before the flood
2001	September 11 - World Trade Center bombed George Bush inaugurated	Roy died from leukemia Nov 1st All Saints Day Attended NFR where Roy was included in a tribute to NFR contestants and notables who had passed that year. Dan Mortensen got us seats.
2003	February 1 - Space Shuttle Columbia explodes, 7 astronauts killed March 19 – Iraq war begins	Traded Craig Self-Storage for Economy Mini Storage in Pueblo
2004	Mars Rover lands on Mars	Moved to Pueblo from Colorado Springs to manage EMS

2005	Hurricane Katrina	Judged Will Rodgers Memorial trick riding contest with Tad Griffith in Claremore, OK
	George W Bush starts 2nd term	
2006	Virginia Tech	Sold house and property in Colorado Springs
	US population reached 300 million	Hired Katherine Graham as manager of EMS
	Minimum Wage $5.85	Judged Will Rodgers Memorial trick riding
		Built home in Pueblo
2007	Dubai builds world's tallest building	Judged Will Rodgers Memorial trick riding in Oklahoma
2008	Barack Obama elected President	Linda Crawford joined me in AZ at Bonnie Reynold's for the winter
2009	Ted Kennedy dies, 77 year old	Barrel Race won: NSPRA South West Region Championship; also, ribbon roping

2010	Don't Ask Don't Tell military policy	Barrel Race won NSPRA South West Region Championship Judged trick riding contest put on by Leann Pollack in Toronto, Canada, with my son, Ryan Rodewald
2011	Gabbie Gifford shot, Tucson	Barrel Race won NBHA Sr 2 D World/Sr 1D, CO Open 1D NBHA district 6, Wickenburg Winter Series Spent winter at Grand Oaks in FL near Ryan and family
2013		November - New hip
2014		January - Pony cart wreck in AZ at Bonnie's; broke arm and lost left eye
2023		Sold house in Pueblo Bought House in the Villages, FL Sold Sunset Stables in Pueblo

www.ingramcontent.com/pod-product-compliance
Lightning Source LLC
Chambersburg PA
CBHW042138160426
43200CB00020B/2970